The Rise and Fall of
Generation Now

T0020909

The Rise and Fall of Generation Now

Tim Ingold

polity

First published in 2024 by Polity Press

Polity Press
65 Bridge Street
Cambridge CB2 1UR, UK

Polity Press
111 River Street
Hoboken, NJ 07030, USA

ISBN-13: 978-1-5095-5660-1
ISBN-13: 978-1-5095-5661-8 (pb)

A catalogue record for this book is available from the British Library.

Library of Congress Control Number 2023937146

Typeset in 11 on 14 pt Sabon LT Pro
by Cheshire Typesetting Ltd, Cuddington, Cheshire
Printed and bound in Great Britain by TJ Books Ltd, Padstow, Cornwall

The publisher has used its best endeavours to ensure that the URLs for external websites referred to in this book are correct and active at the time of going to press. However, the publisher has no responsibility for the websites and can make no guarantee that a site will remain live or that the content is or will remain appropriate.

Every effort has been made to trace all copyright holders, but if any have been overlooked the publisher will be pleased to include any necessary credits in any subsequent reprint or edition.

For further information on Polity, visit our website:
politybooks.com

Contents

Figures

Preface

This little book arises out of my participation, over the past few years, in an interdisciplinary Working Group, 'Facing the Anthropocene', organized by Duke University's Kenan Institute for Ethics, with funding from the Henry Luce Foundation. We were tasked, as a group, with addressing some of the more urgent questions posed by the ongoing planetary crisis, such as how we should understand our own humanity in a milieu that includes so many more ways of being alive than ours, what systems of distribution and democratic governance could rise to these critical times, and what assumptions we would need to revisit, about species and nature, politics and agency, economics and value, in order to restore justice to a world that has tipped so cruelly off balance. In the course of our discussions, I became increasingly convinced that the root of much of our difficulty in facing the future lies in the way we think about generations. We are quick to treat each generation as its own layer, in command of the present, having supplanted its predecessor but destined to be supplanted in its turn. Historically, this way of thinking is anomalous, yet it is nowadays mostly taken for granted as an unquestioned backdrop to discussions of evolution, life and death, longevity, extinction, sustainability, education, climate change, and a host of other matters of intense contemporary concern.

In this book, I suggest a return to the older idea that life is not confined within generations but forged in the collaboration of their overlap. It is by living and working together along the ways of ancestors, I argue, that generations secure a future for themselves and for their descendants. We have reason to be respectful towards those who have worked so hard, and put so much life and soul, into creating a world for us to inhabit. We owe our very existence to their labours, just as those who come after us will owe their existence to ours. Would we not wish the same respect from them? Life is like a relay, and so long as it is carried on, there is hope for generations to come. I have tried in these pages to develop a conceptual vocabulary which would help us give voice to this hope. Many of its keywords are disarmingly simple and of great antiquity; perhaps it will come as no surprise, moreover, that their grammatical form is predominantly that of the verb. They include: to come and to long (from which we get 'becoming' and 'belonging'), to age and to beget, to lean and to last, to care and to attend, to unearth and to undergo, and behind all these, to human. All are words of process.

To forestall any possible misapprehension, however, let me be clear what this book is *not*. For one thing, it is not an ethnographic or sociological study, documenting and analysing the experience of any particular generation, in any specific period or region of the world, or charting the fortunes of its population. My concern is more philosophical: it is with the *idea* of generation, and with how it might be thought otherwise. The Generation Now of my title, then, is the idea a generation has of itself from the act of staking a claim to the present. We can therefore understand its rise and fall in two senses. First, if every Generation Now takes its turn on stage to be in charge of the affairs of the day, then it must have risen to this station in life, and is bound to fall again on making way for its successor. But second, the idea itself has a historical trajectory, rising in tandem with the idea of progress as part of that great project of European thought known as the Enlightenment, but now falling again as the project itself, beset by the multiple social and environmental crises it has set in train, crumbles into disarray.

For another thing, this is not a book about gender. Indeed, I scarcely touch upon the topic. I take 'engendering', here, in its primary sense of begetting, of bringing forth new life, rather than in the secondary sense of investing this life with male or female qualities. Readers so inclined may well detect intimations of femininity in the mutuality of bearing and being borne, and of caring and being cared for, that begetting entails. And they may likewise find intimations of masculinity in the determination of Generation Now to seize the opportunities of the present, in order, as those in its vanguard would say, to 'make history'. They would not be wrong to do so. But I would venture that this is not because generational relations are fundamentally gendered but, to the contrary, because our own understandings of gender are deeply inflected by the way we think about generations. Changing the latter could therefore have profound consequences for the former. To put it more strongly, there can be no justice in gender relations until the injustices built into the predominant model of generational replacement and succession, particularly towards the young and the elderly, are addressed and resolved. That's what I attempt in this book. To explore the consequences of rethinking generations for the ways we think about gender would indeed be a logical next step. I am happy, however, to leave this challenge to scholars better qualified than myself to undertake it.

I offer my thoughts in this book as modest suggestions, rather than grand theory. I do not pretend that they are fully coherent and watertight, or even particularly original. They nevertheless reflect a feeling that has been growing on me for some time. I am persuaded that we need an alternative approach to generations, not just to ameliorate some of our anxieties for times to come, but, more profoundly, to lay a lasting foundation for coexistence. I admit that the approach I propose would mean having to abandon some of our most cherished convictions, including our faith in the inevitability of progress, and in the ability of science and technology to cushion humanity from environmental impacts. I do not believe that a perfect world is just around the corner, or that a day will dawn when our troubles come to an end. But, rather than blaming these troubles on the mistakes of predecessors, only to start over again, I think we might do better to bring generations together once more in the ongoing conversations of life. The message of this book is that life is not – or at least not primarily – about shooting at targets. It is about muddling along, in the gap between means and ends. This is where all possibility lies. In the midst of it all, we don't see a future heading towards us but one that extends as far as we can see. It moves as we do. We'll never get there. But so long as we can keep on going, there is reason for hope.

It remains for me to thank the Henry Luce Foundation for its generous financial support, and Norman Wirzba, in particular, for his steadfast encouragement. The confidence of Ellen MacDonald-Kramer, of Polity Press, in the merits of the project has kept me going throughout. The book has benefited from the comments of two anonymous reviewers. I dedicate the book to my ancestors, without whose labours I would not be here to write it, and offer it to my descendants, with the wish that it may give them succour in troubled times.

Tim Ingold, Aberdeen, January 2023

1

Generations and the Regeneration of Life

The rope and the stack

Imagine you are making rope. For your raw material, you have harvested a quantity of long meadow grass. The rope is formed through a double movement, first by twisting stems of grass, aligned along their length, into strands, and then by twisting the strands around one another. The key thing is that the second twist should be contrary to the first. This ensures that the torque of the individual strands, which would otherwise cause them individually to unwind, only tightens the twist of their winding together, while the torque of the latter, in turn, tightens the twist of each strand. These countervailing forces, along with the friction of longitudinal alignment of the stems themselves, both prevent the rope from unravelling and give it its tensile strength. No grass stem, of course, is more than so long. But by paying new stems into the twist as old ones begin to give out, the rope itself can wind on indefinitely – or at least for as long as your supply of material lasts. If it runs out, you may have to wait another season, for more to grow. Then, with a new harvest, you can pick up again from where you left off.

Now imagine that each stem of grass is a life. It need not be a human life, but let us suppose for the moment that it is. As we know from experience, human lives are generally lived not in isolation but in the company of others. They go along together and, especially in more intimate settings such as of home and family, they twist around one another. And these intimate gatherings, in turn, revolve around one another in the wider circulations of social life. Each winds the other up, lending social life a certain cohesion, and preventing it from fraying. The inclination of particular lives to go their separate ways exerts a friction that tightens the bonds of community; while, conversely, any loosening of communal bonds tightens the intimacy with which these lives rub along. The counterpoint of tension and friction – what the Ancient Greeks called harmony (*armonia*) – holds it all together. No one, of course, lives forever. But as fast as some age and eventually give out, others are born and entered into the twist. Thus, despite the turnover of individual participants, social life can carry on indefinitely, with a rhythm born of the cycle of human generations.

The analogy, to be sure, is not perfect. Perhaps the most critical difference between the rope and social life is that the first is made from materials already gathered, whereas the second makes itself as it goes along, from lives ever growing from the tip. They might be better likened to vines or creepers, each winding around the others as it makes its way through a dense tangle of vegetation. As with the latter, new lives are not introduced from without – as are stems in making rope – but are born from within, in much the same way as, prior to harvesting, new shoots are born from old stems. Nevertheless, I find the image of the rope a helpful place to start in thinking about the *generation* of social life. That's the subject of this book. My questions are simple. What, in the passage of generations, comes before, and what after? Are ancestors in front or behind; descendants behind or in front? How does social life secure its own continuity, or perdure? The answers, however, are of the utmost consequence, not least at a time when this continuity, or perdurance, seems under threat as never before.

I believe this threat, or at least our perception of it, has much to do with a pronounced tendency in modern times to switch focus from the generation of social life to *generations*. What a difference the plural makes! Generation is a process – a bringing forth of life, not just at conception or birth but in every moment of existence. Living, as we shall see, is what we do, but it is also what we undergo as, winding along together, we actively generate ourselves and one another. But generations, in the plural, are like slices that cut across the life process: every generation is a cohort of humanity that has fallen into rank at a particular time, or over a particular interval, whose members judge themselves or are judged in some sense to be coeval, and whose formation is complete at the outset. And in the march of cohorts, we witness not continuity but serial replacement, as each in turn takes the stage and, having enjoyed its share of the limelight, is overlain by its successor and sinks into the past. Generation carries on, but generations pile up, stage by stage, layer upon layer, into a stack.

This kind of stratigraphic thinking is deeply seared into modern sensibilities, and leads to an easy equation of generational layers with layers of sedimentation in the history of the earth, of deposits in the occupation of an archaeological site, of documents in an archive, even of consciousness in the human mind. It is a way of thinking that has worked itself, often without our noticing, into every sphere in which human pasts and futures are at stake, whether in concerns about tradition and heritage, conservation and extinction, sustainability and progress, or art and science. In the following chapters, we will see how it has done so. In every case, substituting the metaphor of the rope for that of the stack casts these concerns in an entirely different light. For whereas, with the stack, as we see in Figure 1.1, every generation

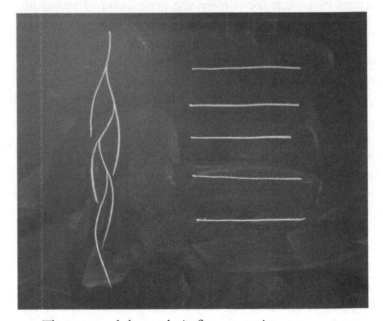

1.1 The rope and the stack, in five generations

is set to replace its predecessor, with the rope young lives overlap older ones, and life itself is regenerated in their collaboration. Nor is this collaboration confined to human lives, since it extends to relations among living beings of every complexion. Only by rethinking generation along these lines, I contend, can we fashion a lasting foundation for coexistence.

Filiation

According to the book of Genesis, it all began with Adam. 'This is the book of the generations of Adam', proclaims the opening line of the book's fifth chapter. At the great age of 130, Adam begat his son Seth, though he still lived for another eight centuries, and went on to beget many more sons and daughters. During all this time, Adam and Seth carried on their lives together. At 105, Seth begat his son Enos, but he too lived for another 807 years before he died. And so it went on: Enos begat Cainan, who begat Mahalaleel, who begat Jared, who begat Enoch, who begat Methuselah, who begat Lamech, who begat Noah.[1] Each of these named characters, except Seth, was a first-born, and went on to enjoy an extraordinarily long life, begetting abundant sons and daughters. These were men of might and renown, and their numerous descendants multiplied on the face of the earth. Yet it was filled with violence and corruption. What happened next is not my concern here. My attention is rather drawn to the slightly archaic verb, 'to beget'. What does it mean, exactly, for one human being to beget another?

Literally, it is to set a new life in train. It is for the one to bring the other into existence with the promise

_____

that the latter, when their time comes, will do the same again. There is a sense, here, of life being handed on in the manner of a relay, kept going by the fresh momentum that newcomers can impart, even as the energies of forerunners begin to fade. In a relay, the baton passes from hand to hand with no change of direction, quite unlike the kind of changing hands that happens, for example, when goods are bought and sold or, as we shall see, when they are inherited. Crucial to begetting, in other words, is that it belongs to the same movement of life as the life it begets. It is a carry-on, not a crossover. And, as such, it is not instant but temporal. Begetting may begin in sexual congress, but this is only the commencement of a process that endures, above all in the everyday work of nurturance and care through which parents *bear* and *raise* their offspring, and the latter theirs. It is a labour of carrying and lifting.

The story of Adam and his descendants, while relentlessly patriarchal, is far from unique. Many peoples around the world take pride in reciting lengthy genealogies, extending from founding ancestors to generations alive today. Often, as in the biblical case, the list follows the male line, but some societies trace it through women, while others keep parallel lists of male and female lines. Common to every such list, however, is that it is compounded of tales of begetting and being begotten. Anthropologists call this 'filiation', the fundamental relation of parent and child. The word comes from the Latin *filius* and *filia*, respectively son and daughter. Both, however, are personalized derivatives of *filium*, meaning 'thread'. Every begetting thus introduces a new thread. Brought forth in the labour of parturition, it proceeds to wind around the parental threads as they carry on together, only to spin new threads as old ones give way. Filiation, then, is an entwining of threads. And to recite a genealogy, by listing its names, is to follow the twine. Indeed, naming is itself part of the process of begetting, of introducing the person and indexing their affiliations. Every name, in its enunciation, becomes part of the story.[2]

Consult any classic anthropological text on the subject of kinship and descent, however, and this is not how filiation is depicted. Such texts are full of genealogical charts in which persons are conventionally represented by means of miniature icons: triangles for males and circles for females. If the chart is intended to depict a relation that is indifferent to the gender of those it links, convention dictates a diamond.[3] A straight line connecting any two icons then depicts the relation: horizontal if of the same generation, such as siblings from the same union; vertical if of successive generations. Filiation, then, appears as a straight, vertical line, connecting parent (mother or father) and child (boy or girl). You can see this in the diagram on the left of Figure 1.2. But the line drawn here is not a line of life. On the contrary, the life of every person is condensed – in the diagram as on a typical kinship chart – into a point, be it shaped as a circle, triangle or diamond. This point is immobile, fixed into place by its position in the genealogical frame. And the line, even as it connects points, marks their irrevocable separation.

There is no begetting here, no relay-like carry-on from one life to the next. For as long as they live, the distance between parent and child remains constant. Whatever practical or affective contact they have during their lives will neither bring them closer together, nor drive

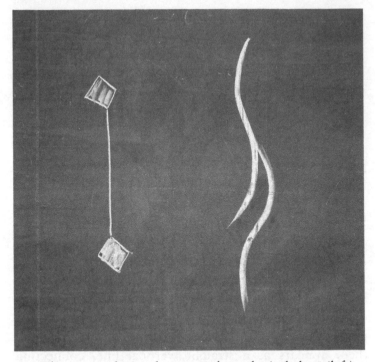

1.2 Filiation: as depicted on an anthropological chart (left), and as one thread of life issuing from another (right)

them farther apart. They are where they are, located by a calculus that determines their position independently of their lifetime comings and goings. This is the calculus of relatedness. When we say that parent and child are related, in this sense, it tells us nothing about the quality of their relationship, or about how they carry on their lives together. It tells us only that certain attributes or properties of the parent are replicated in those of the child. Compare this to the diagram on the right in Figure 1.2, which shows the life of the child issuing from that of its parent in a relation of filiation that continues for the duration of their overlap. Here there is no gap to cross. Rather, the growing distance between child and parent is a function of the gradual diminution of affective contact as one, outliving the other, goes on to bind with its own offspring.

The genealogical model

Let me return to the metaphors of the rope and the stack. With the rope, as we've seen, life is carried on over generations. Indeed, with so many overlapping threads, it is impossible to say at what point one generation ends and another begins. All we can say is that, after enough time has elapsed, every single one of the threads that were once running together have given way to those more recently introduced. The rope itself continues. But with the stack, the life of every generation is confined to its own layer. Gradually, as its potential is exhausted, a new layer crystallizes above it, and then another, and so on. Renewal can come only from superimposition, from adding another layer to the stack. With each additional layer, earlier ones drop down. What, then, passes from one layer and the next? Not life, but resources – whether material or informational – for living it. In slicing one generation from the next, the metaphor of the stack introduces a fundamental discontinuity, cutting off the life that goes on within generations from the transfer of resources between them. This cut lies at the foundation of what I shall henceforth call the *genealogical model*.

It is one thing, of course, to model genealogies; quite another to perform them. People who recite the names and deeds of forebears, listing who begat whom and celebrating their exploits, tell an unbroken story leading from their founding ancestors to those alive today. The model, however, recasts the story as a sequence of discrete but related episodes.[4] We could think of these episodes as making up a series in which each begins not with the story so far, but with a script written from fragments of the previous one. And the definitive axiom of the genealogical model is that, for every episode, the elements of the script, and the message they embody, should be bestowed *independently and in advance* of the story that subsequently unfolds. Each generation's story is its own, albeit written from materials received from the past, and in turn contributing materials to the future. This episodic recasting is what happens when the life of generations is sliced up, as on an anthropological chart, into a series of strata. But it is a move by no means confined to anthropology. We find it in biology too, in its modelling of the genealogy of life.

Ever since Charles Darwin proposed his theory of variation under natural selection to account for how species undergo adaptive modification along lines of descent, evolutionary biologists have assumed that every organism lives to be itself, to act out an episode coextensive with its own life cycle. This, its materialization into manifest being, is known as development or *ontogenesis*. But, though it takes its time, ontogenesis unfolds within the episodic present. What the organism contributes to future episodes, according to the theory, is not its life but a suite of characters, transmitted by way of reproduction to its progeny, out of which are assembled scripts for the episodes that they, in turn, will live to enact. Due to accidents of mutation and recombination, individuals are bound to differ in their precise character profile, with consequences for their relative

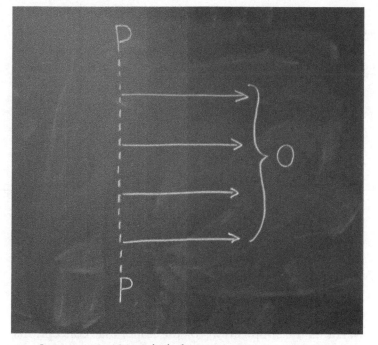

1.3 Ontogenesis (O) and phylogenesis (P)

fecundity. Some characters proliferate in a lineage, while others dwindle or disappear. The resulting changes, compounded over a great many generations, add up to what evolutionary biologists call *phylogenesis*. Thus, as shown in Figure 1.3, whereas ontogenesis is confined within generations, phylogenesis cuts across them. The former is a life process, but not intergenerational; the latter is intergenerational, but not a life process.[5]

This division between ontogeny and phylogeny, however, presupposes some mechanism for copying the elements of a script across from one generation to the next *that is independent of the life-historic episodes which, in various combinations, they are expected to deliver*. For evolutionary biologists of the mid twentieth century, finding this mechanism was tantamount to a quest for the Holy Grail, which would finally unlock the secrets of life. With the discovery of the structure of the DNA molecule, many believed it had at last been found. The apparent capacities of this remarkable molecule not only to encode information in its extended sequence of nucleotides, but also to make almost perfect copies of itself within the matrix of the cell, fitted the bill precisely. With that, the rather abstract, quasi-mathematical exercise of genealogical modelling took on the concrete mantra of a laboratory science. For its advocates, the so-called neo-Darwinian synthesis of natural selection theory and population genetics was finally vindicated. So certain were they, indeed, that one of their number, Nobel Prize-winning biochemist Jacques Monod, could declare, in a book first published in 1970, that 'nothing warrants the supposition (or the hope) that conceptions about this should, or ever could, be revised'.[6]

Yet nothing in neo-Darwinian theory mandates that DNA replication is the only way to copy characters across life cycles. Psychologists, keen to extend neo-Darwinian principles to cover the rudiments of culture, would go on to note that – in humans especially, but to a lesser extent in other animals – certain elements of the script to be copied may be encoded not in molecules but in words or equivalent symbols, or even in behaviours. To explain how these elements get to be replicated in successive generations, however, they needed a theory of learning. Students of animal behaviour had heretofore treated learning largely as an aspect of ontogenetic development. The animal, they supposed, learns in its own generation by adjusting its behaviour through practice and experience in an environment. But to copy information *across* generations by other-than-genetic means, independently of the conditions of life, required a mechanism of an entirely different kind. Echoing the division between phylogeny and ontogeny, psychologists would call it 'social learning', as distinct from the 'individual learning' of lifetime experience. While an individual learns throughout its life, they claimed, by *emulating* others, social learning takes place by way of *imitation*.[7] And underwriting the distinction is the very same logic, of the genealogical model.

Inheritance and perdurance

One generation, according to this logic, cannot beget another. Begetting, as we've already seen, belongs to the same movement of life as the life it begets. It is a carry-on. With the logic of the genealogical model, however, generational succession intersects this movement. What each generation accordingly receives from its predecessor is not its life but a legacy. In a word, it *inherits*. And a condition of inheritance is that whatever is conveyed thereby is broken off from the life of the legator and is passed across, or literally *transmitted*, to the legatee. In law, this could include land, property or title, though in popular usage the concept of inheritance was readily extended to features of physiognomy or temperament, allegedly derived from a parent or ancestor. A child might thus 'inherit' their father's temper or their grandmother's eyes. Only later did the term enter the formal languages of biology and psychology to describe the cross-generational recurrence of manifest characteristics, otherwise known as *traits*. Strictly speaking, however, traits are not received intact and ready-made at the start of every life cycle, but are developed anew in each. Traits, in short, are not themselves heritable. What, then, *do* individuals inherit?

Biologists would answer by positing a concept of the gene. If traits are not received intact at the point of transfer, then, barring accidents of mutation, the genes for building them *are*, allegedly encoded in the molecular materials of heredity. Psychologists would follow suit, by inventing a parallel concept of the meme, conceived as a particle of information transmitted not genetically but by imitation. Some, with great fanfare, would propose synthetic models of 'gene–culture co-evolution', proceeding through variation and selection along twin tracks of inheritance – respectively, genetic and memetic.[8] Manifest traits, then, are the combined output of genes and memes. Not content with this, others have proposed yet a third track, of 'ecological inheritance', working in tandem with the other two. Their argument is that organisms don't merely adapt to environments as they find them; they modify their environments through activities of 'niche construction' – as beavers build dams for example, or as human farmers clear land for cultivation – and these modifications, outlasting their makers, are also handed down to offspring as part of their conditions of life. As ontogenesis is divided from phylogenesis, and emulation from imitation, so, in this view, niche construction occurs within generations, ecological inheritance between them.[9]

There is an element of magical thinking in this appeal to inheritance, whether genetic, cultural or ecological. For it conjures forms and meanings from thin air, as if they were available for transmission independently of

the very processes that give rise to them.[10] Molecules
of DNA, for example, encode nothing in themselves.
If there is a message in the genes, it can be read only
retroactively, from ensuing developmental outcomes.
Likewise, words and other behavioural signs don't come
with meanings pre-attached, as meme-theory supposes;
rather, they gather their meanings in use, from their
effects in the world. As Ludwig Wittgenstein put it, in
his *Philosophical Investigations*, they are like tools in a
tool-box.[11] You have to learn to use them. For appren-
tices learning a trade, this doesn't mean trying out, in
solitary practice, an already acquired operative schema.
They have, rather, to work alongside the master – the
one demonstrating a task, the others closely observing
and co-ordinating their movements with their obser-
vations so as to get the feel of things for themselves.
Imitation and emulation, here, are one and the same.
Skills cannot therefore be inherited. They can only be
produced and reproduced in the course of intergenerational collaborative work.

So, too, with modified environments. Human farmers, as we've seen, are niche constructors par excellence.
Suppose, then, that you are from a farming family.
Generations of your ancestors have worked the farm,
which you now stand to inherit under terms set out in
title deeds. What these documents describe, however,
is a legal fiction. As a landed estate, it is presented as
a property of measurable extent. But, having worked
alongside your parents and grandparents in the fields,
you know that the *real* farm is not like that. It is rather
a matrix of earth and crops which, if it is to bear fruit
now and for generations to come, calls for unceasing
attention, year in, year out. The work is never finished.

Inheritance alone holds no promise of intergenerational stability, when a prodigal heir could allow the farm to go to rack and ruin. Judged by the integrity of the buildings, the condition of the fields and the efficiency of drainage, stability has actively to be sustained through productive work. What keeps the farm going as a habitable and productive environment is not, after all, the inheritance of its assets but the continuity of the agricultural labour process.

In practice, then, neither life-skills nor productive environments are inherited. Rather, they perdure. Where inheritance cuts across from one generational life cycle to another, perdurance is a life process that carries on in the overlap of generations. In perdurance, as philosopher Henri Bergson put it, we see 'each generation *leaning over* the generation that shall follow'.[12] We see it in work on the farm, in apprenticeship, in the love of parents for their children, in the labours of begetting. Herein, for Bergson, lies the essence of life, the *élan vital*. To a Darwinian mainstream deceived by its own magic into believing that generations, set apart by the very bonds of inheritance that connect them, cannot enter affectively into each other's formation – and that affect is therefore confined to individual experience – the *élan vital* is a dangerous delusion. To us, however, it signals the return from inheritance to begetting, from the march of generations to the regeneration of life. Every individual organism, in Bergson's inimitable words, 'is merely a bud that has sprouted on the combined body of both its parents'.[13] From its body will sprout others, as life endlessly winds on. We are back, at last, with the rope.

2

Modelling the Human Life Course

Ageing and begetting

Does life take you any nearer to your ancestors, or does it draw you ever farther away from them? Do you follow in their footsteps or face determinedly in the other direction? Are your ancestors ahead of you, beckoning you on towards the future, or are they left behind, receding ever farther into the past? And your descendants? Are they at your heels, or have they already overtaken, leaving you trailing in their wake? Which way is younger, and which older? These are perplexing questions. I have already compared the passage of generations to the winding rope, of which every life is a strand. Let us commence our inquiry, then, from this analogy. We might allow the rope to run through our fingers, at least so far as it has been wound until now, reciting the names of ancestors in succession as we tell the story of who begat whom. The names are strung along, with earliest ancestors in the lead, followed by later ones. The rope is, quite literally, a *record*: memory rewound. And surely, you observe, the narrative runs as life does, from past to present, and will continue into the future as the rope winds on.

That may indeed be how it looks from the outside. What would happen, however, if you took up a perspective from within? Imagine yourself as one of the strands. As you proceed through life, ageing as you go, you leave a trail behind you. Picture the trail as a string of footsteps, spooling out from beneath your feet, with your earliest steps farthest in the rear, followed by later ones. Always ahead of you are your forebears, who have handed the baton to you to carry on in the same direction. They are already now where you will be, standing for the future towards which you are heading. And behind come your offspring, now stepping where you once were, so long ago. They stand for the past. In the interval between them lies the ageing process. This process, however, is proceeding in a direction contrary to that of the genealogical narrative. For your ancestors are now before you and your descendants at your back. It is as though you were standing in a queue, which is ever shuffling forward as the rope continues to wind. As I have tried to show in Figure 2.1, *ageing is the inverse of begetting.*

The etymology of the word 'queue' offers a clue to this reversal of perspective. Derived from the Latin *cauda*, meaning 'tail', it was initially extended to refer to the stalks of plants and to plaits of twisted hair, and thence to people standing in line to take their turn. Thus, just as ageing inverts begetting, the queue inverts the tail. Place yourself, then, in the queue, with your predecessors ahead and successors behind. Not all these people, of course, may still, or yet, be alive and present

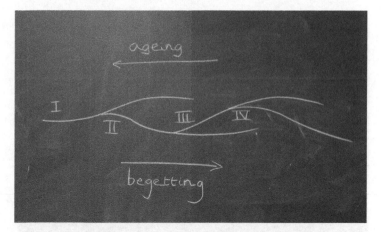

2.1 Ageing and begetting (Roman numerals indicate successive filiations)

in the immediately sensible world. But even those who have 'passed', as we might say – if only from the perspective of an onlooker – continue to exert a hold over their followers, who are beholden to them, even as those who have yet to be born will be beholden to yourself and your contemporaries. The ancestors still beckon, even as you await the coming of descendants. In the meantime, and like everyone else, you process through life, measuring out your days in steps towards a future which, like a spatial horizon, nevertheless recedes as fast as you approach it. Suppose, however, that you are commanded to turn around, through 180 degrees. What then?

Everything changes. For the people who once went before you are now at your back, while you now find yourself face to face with those who were once following after. The future, which had formerly stretched away into the distance along ancestral paths, as sketched in

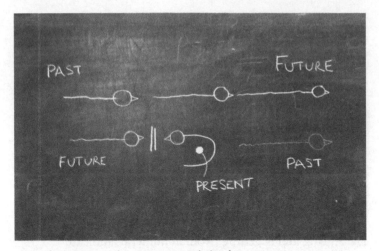

2.2 The turn on the present and the future's past

the top row of Figure 2.2, now appears to be heading on a collision course straight towards you. Meanwhile the ancestors, upon whom you have now turned your back, recede ever farther into the past. Their time is over. The very act of conversion, shown in the bottom row of the sketch, *stakes a claim for the present*. The present is a hold-up, an attempt to arrest the passage of time, to bring it to a standstill. But no generation can hold its ground indefinitely. Eventually, the press becomes too great, and it is either pushed aside or forced to move on, to make way for the next generation, which promptly does the same, turning its back on the one preceding only to face its own successor. The moment it turns, it takes the stand of a new present. History, then, reappears as a punctuated series of generational turning points, each claiming the present for itself.

To join the queue is to observe what we rightly call a tradition. For the proper meaning of tradition – from the Latin *tradere*, to 'hand over', as in a relay – is not to live in the past but to follow your predecessors into the future. You may retrace old ways, but every trace is an original movement to be followed in its turn. It is the same with storytelling, in which the direction of live performance is inverted in the temporal flow of the narrative. Even as the words fall from your lips, they recede into the slipstream of your onward movement. Strictly speaking, then, to turn your back on tradition is not to relinquish what is already past. It is rather to deny the promise that tradition offers for the future. In other words, the 'pastness' of tradition is not given a priori, but is produced in the very act of conversion that stakes a claim to the present. This same turnaround, moreover, creates a future which, from the perspective of those still following traditional ways, is nothing if not backward-looking, sacrificing the possibility of ceaseless beginning for the finality of predetermined ends. Such is the way of modernity.

The Angel of History

This is a way that measures time by the clock. Why, after all, does the clock tick? Its revolving movement, driven by the vital force of the spring which wants always to unwind, or the weight of the pendulum as it gravitates to earth, is periodically stopped on the cog of an escapement wheel by a ratchet, only to be released again. The tick we hear is the sound of the ratchet's engagement with the cog. And the measured time of the clock lies not in the unwinding of the spring but in the series of stoppages, each marked by a tick. So, likewise, as diagrammed schematically in Figure 2.3,

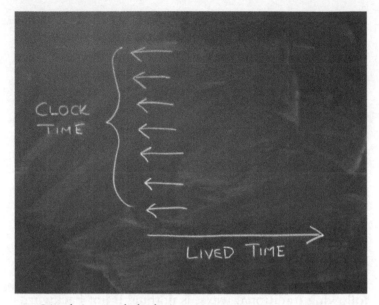

2.3 Lived time and clock time

do generations mark time by converting its onward movement into a punctuated series of escapements. With life, as with time, the flow becomes a stutter. When life escapes, the entire series shifts by one notch. The foregoing generation, far from moving on into the future, vanishes into the oblivion of the past, while the generation to come pivots to take its place in the present. Thus does every present generation, having turned its back to the past, position itself as a gatekeeper to the future.

That's why there is such a compulsion to replace the old with the new: it proves that time is passing and history is being made. Nothing, indeed, catches the modern imagination more than the idea of step change. For, in the eyes of the present, the future figures less as a path to be followed than as a problem to be solved. Had it been solved by preceding generations, now already past, there would be nothing for the present to do. They would have only to fall into line with a project mapped out for them in advance. Such compliance would amount to the renunciation of any future they could call their own. The present's ownership of the future, therefore, depends on the assumption that the past got it wrong. This is the default assumption of the modern age: that the road from the past is paved with errors. We always know better than they did. In science and technology, we will refute their conjectures to replace them with inventions of our own. In architecture, we will abandon their designs in favour of the latest innovations. In education, we will cast aside the old order and induct students into the new.

Yet the inevitable implication is that the solutions of the present will turn out in due course to have been equally mistaken. And while the generation that proposes these solutions – that is, our generation – will pass, the impacts of applying them can linger, as have the applications of generations preceding, leaving long-lasting scars not just on hearts and minds, but on the world around us. Every generation, then, is fated to live among the ruins of the now obsolete futures proposed by generations past, perhaps only half-constructed before being demolished to make way for the next. If you were a celestial being, eternally standing guard at the gate at which these erstwhile futures pass, one by one, into history, you would witness an immense pile-up as future after future, crashing into the present, is reduced to rubble. You would be the personification of *Angelus Novus*, The Angel of History, as famously depicted in a monoprint by the artist Paul Klee, dating from 1920, reproduced in Figure 2.4. A year later, the print was purchased by the philosopher-critic Walter Benjamin, and in a fragment penned in 1940, shortly before his own suicide as a fugitive from Nazism, Benjamin described the Angel thus:

> His face is turned toward the past. Where we perceive a chain of events, he sees one single catastrophe which keeps piling wreckage upon wreckage and hurls it in front of his feet. The angel would like to stay, awaken the dead, and make whole what has been smashed. But a storm is blowing from Paradise; it has got caught in his wings with such violence that the angel can no longer close them. The storm irresistibly propels him into the future to which his back is turned, while the pile of debris before him grows skyward. This storm is what we call progress.[1]

The sense of despair is palpable. Can there be any respite from the cataclysmic chain of ultimate solutions that generation after generation has inflicted, all in the name of progress? So long as we seek to shape a future perceived as coming towards us, by projecting our designs onto a world our successors are about to enter, the answer can only be 'no'. We would be fated to the endless stuttering of the escapement mechanism. Stuttering, after all, is not a sign that progress is faltering; it is rather the way progress works, by the serial accumulation of backward movements. Why else, along with the clock, are its iconic instruments the excavator and the crane? The excavator empties the ground of the residues of past interventions, leaving none to pick up and follow; the crane lifts new ones into place from above. Yet the Angel gazes towards ancestral ways. He

2.4 *Angelus Novus*, monoprint by Paul Klee (1920);
courtesy of The Israel Museum, Jerusalem; photo
© The Israel Museum, Jerusalem, by Elie Posner

longs to regain the path of tradition, with its promise of
renewal for a future everlasting. To 'awaken the dead',
for Benjamin, is precisely that: to undo the catastrophic
turn of modernity and be guided once more by the light
and lives of those who have gone before.

What if we were to follow the Angel's gaze? He may seem to face the past, with his back to the future, but that is only from the point of view of we who, having pivoted on the present, cast the future as a project. The Angel himself stakes no claim for the present, but yearns for a time wherein every moment would be the future's past. Dismayed by the turn of events, his staring eyes admonish us to face in the same direction as our ancestors, rather than back to back. In overlapping our lives with theirs, we could work together with them, not against them, to find a path forward. Critically, this is not a recipe for regression or inertia. People who continue to follow their ancestors are not backward. All too often, the belief that they are stuck in the past, left behind by history, has been adduced to justify their oppression – or worse, annihilation. It is a belief that comes, as we have seen, from putting tradition behind us. To join *with* tradition, facing frontward, promises otherwise: to open a future that, far from converging on any projected end, contains within itself the promise of eternity.

The bell-curve

Any generation that seizes the present for itself obstructs the steady progression, in ageing, from past to future. It throws an impenetrable barrier, by order, across the queue, bisecting it at right angles. Young and old now find themselves irrevocably divided on opposite sides. For the young, the present holds up their coming; for the old, it recasts their passing as a retreat. This separation of young and old, I believe, is one of the great tragedies of the modern age. Perhaps it has taken the years of the global pandemic, peaking from 2020 to 2022, to bring the scale of the tragedy home to us. Severe restrictions imposed during periods of lockdown often left the very young and very old in isolation, unable to meet in person. Births remained uncelebrated, and deaths unmourned. But the emergency only highlighted divisions already there. For, more often than not, grandparents and grandchildren would be living far apart, in separate households, even institutions, visiting only intermittently to renew their contact. It is as though a wedge had been driven between them. That wedge is the generation of the present. Thrust between youth and old age, it is what I shall henceforth call 'Generation Now'.

The people of Generation Now are in charge. Having taken possession of their own slice of time and history, they are so busy with their world-making, so preoccupied with the affairs of the day, that they pay scant regard to their elders or to their juniors. Their elders, they think, having already enjoyed their place in the sun, should fade away gracefully into years of decline. Their juniors, to the contrary, need to be brought up to speed, to face a future already prepared for them. The result is to give a peculiar inflection to the life course. It appears to be shaped, as in Figure 2.5, rather like a bell-curve, roughly divisible into three phases. In the first phase, the capacities of young minds are both formed and filled with what they need to know in order to function in the new world they are about to encounter. In the second, intermediate phase, world-forming powers are at their peak. Everyone is hard at work, 'fulfilling their potential', as they like to say. But once this potential is exhausted, having nothing further to deliver, they enter the final phase, of deterioration and decline, as their

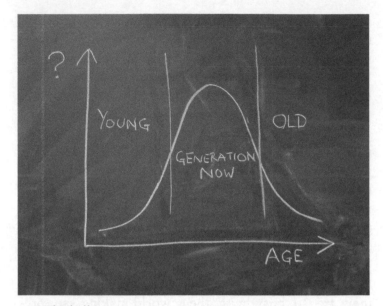

2.5 The bell-curve

capacities fade and their knowledge becomes increasingly obsolete.[2]

What is measured by the height of the curve from the base? Intellectual prowess? The conversion of potential into effective power? Knowledge? It could be all these things. One thing the curve does not measure, however, is wisdom. As we shall see later,[3] there is wisdom in *not*-knowing. The wise may not know, but they can *tell*, in both its senses: their attention is finely tuned to variations in the environment that matter to their ways of living, and they are well versed in the stories of the world, including above all those of the ancestral beings whose activities gave the world its present form. Among peoples we would nowadays call 'indigenous' – but who long ago would have included almost everyone whose living was drawn from the earth and its waters – youngsters would grow up hearing the stories and observing the practices of their elders, discovering the meanings of the stories and developing skills of attention in the passage of their own experience, and becoming storytellers and practitioners in their turn. As we saw in Chapter 1, this is not inheritance but perdurance, as stories are carried on and skills regenerated in the collaboration of generations.

Throughout most of human history, this is precisely how lives have been lived. Old and young would work and age together. Yet, by and large, this is no longer the case today. What happened? What led powerful agents of the intermediate generation forcibly, and sometimes brutally, to cut the rope of begetting, to tear children away from the company of their elders, all in the name of progress? What fired Generation Now with such world-making zeal as to consign the wisdom of its seniors to a bygone past while treating its own juniors as empty vessels, bereft of knowledge, in need of induction into a future they can have no hand in shaping? Answers are not easy to come by. They likely have much to do with capitalism's erosion of domestic modes of production, with the redeployment of educational functions from the family to the state, and, in the case of indigenous peoples, with colonial oppression.[4] What's certain, however, is that Generation Now has little time for stories or for skills. These, it says, are the stuff of tradition, preserved only to entertain the young in enactments of heritage, or to indulge the old in flights of nostalgia.

For Generation Now is target driven. It has its ends and means. Yet, as its ends expand, fuelled by ambitions of progressive development, so its means contract.

Its short-term objectives hold no promise that life can endure beyond a future already in its sights. Faced with looming environmental catastrophe, it has no answer save to dream of a permanent geo-technological fix, or of finding new reservoirs on other planets, leaving the bulk of humanity to eke out a living on an irreparably damaged Earth. Every competition has far more losers than winners, and for every individual smart enough to succeed, another thousand will fail. A world that carries on, however, and offers hope for generations to come, cannot be for some but not others, let alone reserved for a select few. It must have room for everyone and every-thing, for all time. There is but one way, I contend, to bring in such a world, and that is by loosening the grip of Generation Now. Can we imagine a society in which the young and the elderly, currently excluded from the tasks of world-making, are once again enabled to col-laborate in forging the conditions of collective life?

Life and death

We could perhaps take a lesson from the Chukchi, a people indigenous to the far north-east of Siberia. The Chukchi language has two words for what we might call 'life' or 'existence', namely *va'irgin* and *unatgirgin*. Yet their meanings are subtly different. *Unatgirgin* pertains to the beings and things we encounter around us. Each lives, each exists, along its own particular path, carrying on through time like everything else. Yet it exists only as a kind of twist, a coiling over itself, of the everlasting creative movement that is life or existence itself. This latter is *va'irgin*. Without *va'irgin*, as anthropologist Jeanette Lykkegård puts it in her sensitive study of life and death among Chukchi villagers of Aichavayam, in northern Kamchatka, 'there would be no humans, no trees, no rivers, no animals, no sun and so on'.[5] Amidst the force of life (*va'irgin*), things and beings come into presence (*unatgirgin*) for what they are, each with its own form and character. No mortal creature lasts forever, however, and when its time comes, as eventually it must, and provided customary rites are observed, it will melt back into the very flux of creation whence it came, and from which everything originates.

In short, death for the Chukchi is not an end-point; it is a passage into life – or, better, from the realm of the actual into that of the possible. Actual life, like the strand of the rope to which we have already drawn comparison, is full of twists and turns. It coils on itself and around other lives in a spiralling movement that swerves without interruption from the overall direction of flow, forming itself as it goes. Reading Lykkegård's account of the Chukchi lifeworld put me in mind, once again, of the philosophy of Bergson, from which I have derived so much inspiration in the past. It is in the nature of the living, Bergson argued, to 'turn upon themselves'.[6] Life in general moves on, but particular lives always lag behind: they are reluctant, tensing against the flow and winding this tension into their bodily powers so long as they have the stamina to do so, until eventually their strength wanes and, in death, they unwind back into the mainstream. Echoing Bergson, the philosopher Gilbert Simondon would later remark on this capacity 'of falling out of step with themselves', by which living beings resolve themselves into actuality.[7]

This image of falling in and out of step brings back to mind our earlier metaphor of the queue. For

Simondon, as for Bergson, the queue moves on, despite all the twists, turns and missteps of the living. It is from its very momentum, indeed, that creatures draw the energy to generate and sustain their being – or, in a word, for ontogenesis. Likewise for the Chukchi, *unatgirgin* is drawn from *va'irgin*, the actual from the possible. Conversely, actual life harbours an intrinsic drive towards the possibility of death, a progression we experience as ageing. Generation Now, however, as it pivots to stake its claim to the present, brings this entire movement to a juddering halt. Its life, now confined within its own generational layer, is compressed into the equivalent of running on one spot. Faced with the otherwise inevitable prospect of obsolescence and eventual replacement, it does all it can to prolong its hold over the present, seeing ageing as an affront to be resisted. That is why, as Benjamin observes, Generation Now has no envy for the future. Its happiness, he wrote, is steeped in the time assigned to it by the span of its own existence.[8]

Nor does Generation Now have any time for death. It views death not as a movement intrinsic to life, but as an external adversary, attributable to agents of morbidity that have to be staved off by all available means. In the transhumanist dream of immortality, this view is taken to its logical extreme. For transhumanists, death is just another problem to be solved.[9] The fact that every human being alive today is bound to die is merely an index of our technical failure, up to now, to come up with a viable solution. The machinery of the body is still liable to malfunction, and its mental operator inclined to go missing. But if these issues can be fixed, nothing in principle would prevent humans from living forever.

They could say goodbye, once and for all, to the travails of ageing and begetting. This dream is not new; on the contrary, it is inherent in the very idea of progress. In his history of nineteenth-century evolutionary thought, John Burrow has observed how believers in progress would always wish theirs to be the final, or at least the penultimate, generation, 'on the point of opening the last envelope'.[10]

It is quite otherwise for the Chukchi. Ageing and begetting, in their world, are the twin conditions of continuing life. The worst that can befall a person is to die in hospital, not just far from home but in the clutches of a biomedical regime that, in treating death as terminal, irrevocably blocks re-entry into possible life, into *va'irgin*. Yet perhaps even in a society such as ours, with Generation Now firmly in charge, vestiges of possibility remain among both young and elderly, opposite tails of the bell-curve. Alternately 'not yet' and 'already over', they merge in a penumbra surrounding the bright light of the present. Together, grandparents and grandchildren are in touch, in ways that target-driven intermediates of the parental generation are not, with more enduring rhythms of time. This is a time not of diachronic replacement and succession but of continuous renewal, of weather and the seasons, of breaking waves and running rivers, of the growth and decay of vegetation and the coming and going of animals, of breaths and heartbeats. This is the time for which *Angelus Novus* yearns. Were young and old to put their heads together, could they bring it back?

3

Remembering the Way

The laminated ground

When I began as a university lecturer, I considered myself ahead of the curve. I wasn't just teaching new ideas; I was using the latest instrumentation to do so. There were no computers or digital display systems in those days, and even photocopiers were in their infancy. My department, however, had recently acquired a contraption known as an 'overhead projector'. None of my more senior colleagues would touch it, but I was an avid user. I liked to include diagrams in my lectures, and I could prepare by drawing every diagram on a transparent acetate sheet. Placed on the glass of the apparatus with a powerful light shining below and an inclined mirror above, the diagram would be projected onto a big screen for all to see. I could even write on the sheets with a felt pen, either beforehand or as I spoke. Placing the sheets on top of one another, however, produced a peculiar effect. As the lower diagrams showed through, the image that appeared on the screen would be a jumble of criss-crossing lines which bore no more relation to one another than streaks of rain on a windowpane to the textures of the scenery beyond.

Observing a landscape, we typically see a ground likewise crisscrossed with lines of all sorts, including lines of passage like roads, trails, paths and waterways, as well as boundary lines like walls, fences and ditches. Some look to be of considerable antiquity, others more recent or even new. Could it be that this line-crossed ground has been assembled in just the same way as the composition on the overhead projector, through the superposition of multiple layers, each marked up with its own inscriptions? Does the history of a landscape stack up, as every present generation adds its own layer on top of those already laid in the past? Admittedly, the lines of old look faint and, compared with more recent ones, they are hard to discern. Sometimes, they can only be made out from the air. Wondering why this should be so, we might imagine that ground layers are rather less transparent than my acetate sheets. Every additional layer, then, would further obscure its predecessors as the latter sink ever lower in the stack. Nevertheless, as with the projector, the past still *shows through*, albeit dimly – and all the more so under powerful illumination.

We have already found an echo of this idea of a laminated ground in the way anthropology has classically modelled generations and their passage. The same idea crops up in many other fields of humane scholarship. We find it, for example, in studies of language and literature, archaeology and architecture. Linguists distinguish the plane of synchrony from the axis of diachrony, on the first of which is laid out the structural configuration of a language at a given time, and along the second the changes it undergoes as one configuration accedes to the next. In the study of literature, the resemblance of 'genre' and 'generation' is not accidental, as the words share a common root. Theorists analyse how new genres of writing supersede old ones, or how every generation layers its own reading of ancient texts over those of generations past. Archaeologists identify layers in the occupation of a site, each with its distinctive artefact assemblage, and arrayed in a sequence of strata with the most recent on top. Even architects, planning to construct the future rather than uncover the past, tend to suppose that every new project begins with a clean sheet, an immaculate ground on which to build anew.

Behind all these examples lies a now familiar premise – namely, that *life is lived in the present*. We, today's people, live in our time; the people of the past lived in theirs. But it is impossible, according to this premise, for descendant lives to prolong ancestral ones, or for ancestral lives to beget their descendants. Social life may be a long conversation, but for linguists, every utterance in the conversation – in so far as it is governed by a structure common to speakers of the language – takes place on the plane of synchrony. Diachronic change, from one plane to the next, is fundamentally discontinuous. For students of literature, likewise, the text or the reading is an expression of its era; in the literary canon, every genre is a generation, and writing goes on within genres rather than in the process of generating those to come. In the archaeological record, artefacts hold fast to the date of their manufacture, while sinking ever further into the past. They grow older with every passing year, but never age. And in architecture, buildings belong to the centuries of their construction, surviving in the present thanks only to acts of preservation.

This premise, however, is also fundamental to the idea of heritage. Literally, heritage is an inheritance, a legacy that one generation passes on, fully formed and intact, to the next. And, as we've seen, to be inherited this legacy – whether of things or ideas, tangible or intangible – must be broken off from the ebbs and flows of life, and from the histories of place and people of which our own life-stories are the continuation. A life that perdures over generations cannot, by the same token, be inherited. Children do not inherit their parents and grandparents. They may of course inherit parental *property*, including personal effects and prerogatives, along with the ancestral house and the plot of land on which it stands. But they cannot inherit the affective milieu of their upbringing, the home in which they were raised or the place to which it belongs. Likewise, the young may inherit from their elders a wealth of literature, whether oral or written, but not their mother tongue. They cannot inherit kin, affect, home, place or tongue because these things make up the very matrix from which they have grown, and are already part and parcel of who they are.

Pathways from the past

What does it take, then, to turn life into heritage? It is the equivalent of turning persons into properties, affects into effects, homes into houses, place into land, and conversation into text. In every case, it means taking the life out of them, rather than regarding each as an ongoing nexus of growth and development. With this reduction,

---

the person is but a bundle of traits or characteristics, love and care are but the bestowal of material assets, the home is but a building, a place but its physical setting, spoken language but a corpus of expressions. The more life is drained from ancestral ways, in their conversion to heritage, the more it is consequently squashed into the plane of the present. We have already seen this logic at work with the genealogical model, in its absolute severance of the life that goes on within generations from the transmission of resources between them. Once again, we encounter the idea that generations are stacked over one another, each inhabiting its own slice of time, both separated and connected by the transfers of inheritance. What happens, then, when the object of conveyance is the very ground upon which life is lived?

Life generally leaves its mark on the ground in the form of tracks and trails. With bipedal humans, it takes more than one pair – more even than a few pairs – of passing feet to form a trail. A lone human pedestrian leaves only footprints, and then only on soft ground, with spaces between them measured by the walker's gait. A quadrupedal animal, such as a horse or dog, leaves a different but equally recognizable pattern of hoof- or paw-prints. These are tracks, and you can read much from them about the creature that made them – what it was, when it passed, where it was heading and even how fast it was going. But tracks are not trails. To wear a trail, so many feet must pass the same way, whether in one mass movement or in numerous solitary movements over an extended period, that distinct prints are rarely discernible. Thus, the trail is formed along with the beings that walk it, the places they inhabit and the landscape in which it is inscribed, as the crystallization of a collective life process. As such, it may be carried on through generations, as descendants follow in the footsteps of their ancestors.

As a child, you may have walked a familiar path with your parents and grandparents, who may have once walked it with theirs when they were young. The path is something that you and they make together. But precisely because it is continually co-produced in the collaboration of generations, the path is not inherited. Perhaps that's why so few paths, even today, are commemorated as embodiments of heritage.[1] In our everyday experience, to walk a path is, at the same time, to remember how it goes; it is a vital movement of prolongation that anticipates the future even as it trails a storied past. To convert a path into heritage would mean breaking this movement, turning it into an *object* of memory, like a narrative completed, ready to be transferred as any other heritable property. To walk a heritage trail, then, is not to carry on a living tradition but to re-enact a past that is already wrapped up. To return to my comparison with the overhead projector, it is like placing one acetate sheet upon another that is already marked up with a line, and then tracing the same line on the new sheet.

Crucially, in this operation, the traced line overwrites the original *without ever making contact with it.* On the heritage trail, we can never walk in the footsteps of our ancestors, as once we walked with our parents and grandparents, since the logic of inheritance has placed us on separate layers whose surfaces can touch like the pages of a stack, but whose lines can never meet. Perhaps this is the source of the peculiar expression, so popular with policymakers, that every new intervention is not so much to be written out as *rolled out.* If every walk of life is a roll-out, then, far from reinscribing an existing ground, it leaves that ground untouched while layering a new one, to be marked up with its own inscriptions. Yet, except under artificial conditions which carefully protect the heritage path from the wear of passing feet, for example by placing it under glass, this is not what happens in practice. On the contrary, far from adding a new layer, the walker's footprints contribute to its ongoing inscription. Meanwhile, the ground surface itself is continually renewed, not by adding layers but by removing them, by way of natural processes of erosion.

This, finally, is why the analogy with the overhead projector fails. Let me return to the question of why older paths should appear fainter than recent ones. Long ago, when in regular use, these ancient ways would have been deeply etched in the ground. But since then, gradual erosion, principally through weathering, has brought the depths of these inscriptions almost to the surface, soon to disappear. They are scarcely visible. Meanwhile, later paths, yet to suffer prolonged exposure to the weather, have left deeper marks – the most recent, deepest of all. The comparison, in this instance, is not with the overhead projector but with the product of a much earlier technology of writing, with pen on parchment – namely, the palimpsest. This is formed when the same parchment is reused, over and over again. Between every round of inscription, the surface is scraped to remove as much of the previous traces as possible. But some always remain. With the palimpsest, old inscriptions do not lie *beneath* the semi-translucent surface of the present, but rather *rise up* to the surface even as newer writing sinks down. Like the writer's parchment, the ground is renewed not by layering but by overturning.[2]

From archive to anarchive

Where grounds are stacked up, memory figures as an archive. Older memories lie beneath and can be accessed only by stripping away the later ones that time has deposited above, extracting whatever we find there, and appropriating it as an object of heritage. To memorialize the past, then, is to undo the work of time. The future, to the contrary, can only be projected upon a plane of virtual reality, *as if* the surface of the present were already overlain. Thus, for those who have staked a claim to the present, memorialization and projection face in opposite directions, respectively towards a past that is under and a future that is over. But what if the ground doesn't stack but turns? As shown in Figure 3.1, 'under' and 'over' take on different meanings here. In the cycle of turning, under is 'coming up' and over

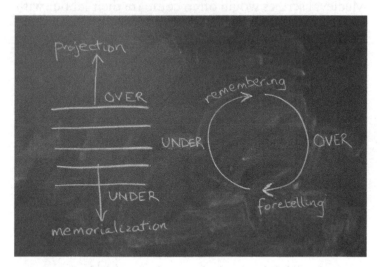

3.1 Over and under, with a stacked ground (left) and a turning ground (right)

41

'going down'. What is over is no longer above, on the virtual plane of the future, but already on its way down, into the past. And what is under is no longer beneath, in the past, but has arisen to the surface of ongoing activity as it heads into the future. It is not under*neath* but under *way*.

We could perhaps compare this turn of the ground to turning the leaf of a book. As you read, following the lines of text, you have periodically to turn over, whereupon the page you had been reading is laid down, allowing the page on the underside to come up. This analogy between ground and page is, indeed, as old as the book. The very word 'page' comes from the Latin *pagus*, meaning an expanse of inhabited countryside with its fields and farms, from which are also derived the English 'peasant' for one who works the land, and the French 'paysage' for the landscape shaped by his efforts. Medieval scribes would often compare their labour with pen on parchment to that of the peasant with his plough, turning the soil. I have already observed, in Chapter 2, that the iconic engines of modernity, besides the clock, are the excavator and the crane. In a layered world, one can either dig down or add from above. But in a world that turns – not with the revolutions of the clock but to the rhythms of the agricultural cycle – inscribing the ground is itself an act of renewal. Its iconic instrument is the plough.

In his *New Science* of 1725, the Enlightenment philosopher Giambattista Vico speculated that the roots of the word 'human' could lie with the Latin *humando*, referring to the funerary rites of burial. Both by origin and destiny, then, humans would be of the soil (*humus*). Most specialists consider Vico's etymology to be fanciful; there is nevertheless some truth to the view, proposed by literary scholar Robert Pogue Harrison, that 'to be human means above all to bury', or to lay what Harrison calls the *humic* foundation for life – a foundation that 'holds in its conserving element the unfinished story of what has come to pass'.[3] Although burial thus turns the page on a life, it is not the end of the story, which it is the task of coming generations to carry on, above all in the labours of begetting and being begotten. Remembering, here, does not undo, but joins *with*, the work of time – of weather and the passage of the seasons – in bringing ancient ways to the surface, so that they may be followed by the living as they fare into the future. It is a process, in a word, of *unearthing*.

By unearthing, I mean the opposite of excavation. To excavate is to empty a deposited past of its contents – literally, to hollow it out. It is what archaeologists do when they cut through the levels of occupation of a site, towards ever deeper strata. For them, the earth is an archive, holding a record of past generations in its sediments, and their aim is to reconstruct the record by extracting its hidden secrets. Among these secrets are the bodies of the long dead. The grave, from this archaeological perspective, is a place of deposition: doubly so, indeed, since bodies already interred at the time of death would have sunk even farther as the grounds of antiquity would themselves have been submerged beneath subsequent layers of historical sediment. Yet a deposit that sinks ever deeper below the surface with the advance of time holds no potential for regeneration. Deposition, thus, is the very antithesis of burial, the purpose of which is to establish a humic foundation for ongoing life, in just the same way as roots or tubers buried below ground hold the promise of vegetative growth. In a nutshell, whereas deposition affords excavation, burial is a condition for unearthing.[4]

The turning ground, then, is the converse of the archive. It is an *anarchive*, to borrow an idea from philosopher Erin Manning. Where the contents of the archive are inert, their potential spent, 'the anarchive' – Manning writes – 'wants to activate, to orient. Or better said, it is always already activating, orienting.'[5] Landscape as anarchive is a riot of subterranean roots and runners, ever issuing above ground into new life. This is how architect Hong Wan Chan describes the landscape of Nanhai, part of the Pearl River Delta in South China, which she knows intimately from her own family history. Once a mesh of villages, fields, pathways and tombs, it is now heavily urbanized. Chan's family had a hillock near her native village which had served as a burial site for generations of her ancestors, and a fount of vitality for the lineage, until it was levelled in the early 2000s to make way for a motorway, requiring the graves to be moved to a formal cemetery. In the cemetery, neatly ordered by the planners of Generation Now, the ancestors are archived, their humic power to activate the landscape truncated to create a *tabula rasa* for urban development.[6]

Longing

No less exuberantly anarchival, but equally vulnerable to levelling, are the tropical forests of Peninsular Malaysia. Their indigenous inhabitants, the Batek, traditionally lived by hunting and gathering. While many still do, commercial felling in the region has made their lives increasingly precarious. For the Batek, however, the forest is not just a storehouse for provisions. It is a lifeworld teeming with memories: of places where they have hunted or fished, or collected rattan, or met this or that person, or where their kinsfolk dwell. Roaming in the forest, as Batek habitually do, these memories keep rising to the surface, and are recounted in the stories they tell. Yet, at times, the subject of the story is beyond reach, particularly when a place evokes the memory of someone who has passed away. The Batek have a word, *haʔip*, for the feeling that wells up on such occasions. Tuck Po Lye, in her study of Batek lifeways, translates the word as 'longing'. One can long for a place far away, a loved one, a deceased elder. Lye recalls one man pointing out a trail to her. 'Old people used to walk there', he said. 'So, when people *haʔip* the dead elders, they return to the trail.'[7]

For Batek people, to journey along a way of life is also to remember those who have gone before. The trails of predecessors, now fading in the undergrowth, are nearest to the surface, and by attending closely one can follow in the elders' wake, knowing however that, like the ends of the rainbow, they will ever remain beyond the horizon. This is what it means to observe a tradition. It is a process of longing, but equally, as it rebounds upon the one who longs, a process of *belonging*. So, too, people of the coming generation, in following the lead of their elders, *become* the persons they are. There can be no becoming without coming; no belonging without longing. Coming and longing, or journeying and remembering, are two aspects of one and the same fundamental movement. Critically, therefore, they face not in contrary directions – respectively, towards the future and towards the past – but *in the same way*. The ancestors we follow are always ahead, beyond our ken. We can grasp them neither physically nor in the categories of thought. We will never reach them, let alone overtake. That's why we long for them.

For us moderns, accustomed to submerging the past beneath the present and erecting the future over it, this might seem a strange conclusion to arrive at. It is hard to divest ourselves of the assumption that remembering is necessarily retrospective. How, we ask, can you possibly project into the future and cast your eye into the past at one and the same time? Would it not require a veritable Janus, with two faces looking simultaneously front and back, to accomplish such a feat? But let us not forget the Angel of History, who, turning his back on the accumulating wreckage of historical progress, pines for a time in which we could once again see a future reaching out along the ways of our ancestors, and every present moment as its past. This is not the diachronic time that ranks generations of history in sequence, above and below. It is a time, rather, that inheres in the ceaseless becoming of the world. '*Wherever anything lives*', wrote the philosopher Bergson, weighing his words with emphasis, '*there is, open somewhere, a register in which time is being inscribed.*'[8] This is the register of longing, and it goes on and on.

One night, another of Lye's elderly Batek companions kept her awake with the story of a journey he had made to visit his grandson, who had been sick. As he went on his way, he was constantly longing for the little boy, who was ever before him in his mind. 'And I walked, walked, walked, I thought. I thought, thought,

thought in my mind, I walked. I walked walked walked, I thought, I thought.'⁹ If he ever arrived, we never hear of it. For longing does not go from a point of departure to a destination. It follows a different axis, of perdurance, seeking not to conjure up the future or to wish back the past, but to align care and attention with the temporal stretch of life. Longing is thus neither utopian nor nostalgic. It affords no final release into the light, as in utopian dreams of a perfect world. But nor does it hanker after a past irretrievably overwritten by the present. Nostalgia is for those who would re-enact an already memorialized heritage as historical pageant. People like the Batek, for whom memory is everywhere in the storied landscape, have no need of it.

Longing, then, does not lead from a dark, subterranean past into the bright light of the future, but feels its way in a twilight zone with no end in sight. It says much about the attitude of Generation Now, however, that it can accommodate the register of longing only by flattening it. Indigenous hunter-gatherers such as the Batek, bereft of targets for the future and with no archive of the past, are allegedly stuck in a time-warp of traditionality that prevents them from ascending even to the first rung of history. They are said to be at once ancient, epitomizing the original, pre-progress state of humanity, and childlike in their innocence of civilization. We are right to dismiss such assertions as instances of ethnocentric prejudice, driven by a colonial mentality. But the prejudice is directed just as much towards other generations. Unfavourable comparisons between indigenous peoples and children or ancients are equally a reflection of Generation Now's disdain for the old and the young, as of its contempt for those it considers 'primitive'. Could a more favourable comparison help to foreground the anarchival powers of an animate landscape that Generation Now has done so much to put down?

4

Uncertainty and Possibility

Lifting the curse

The progressive view of Generation Now casts its projects upon an imagined future, while consigning its forerunners to an archived past. This view, while easy to state, is hard to dislodge. In human history, it is more the exception than the rule, yet it is so deeply embedded in the modern constitution that shifting it will require a wholesale reorientation of our approaches to conservation, development, education and science. This will be my task for later chapters. Suffice it to observe at this point that in every domain of policy and practice, the conceit that we can plan the future from the standpoint of the present has something illusory about it. This is because the direction of projection is contrary to the flow of life. It amounts to a hold-up, which can only be broken by shelving the project and installing another in its place. Continually swimming against the tide, we strive in vain to arrest the flow. To follow the thread of the future's past, to the contrary, means acknowledging

---

that we are ever behind where we will be, and where others have already been. This, as we have seen, was the stance of the Angel of History.

Perhaps we would better compare ourselves to mariners on the high seas. The mariner knows fore from aft, bow from stern, and ploughs a course through the ocean guided by currents, winds, the sun and moon, stars and seabirds. What sensible mariner would place his aft in the future and his bow in the past? Yet this is what we do, whenever we project futures for ourselves. Having turned on the present we walk backwards through life, choosing not to see the future that would otherwise lie before us. We are in denial when it comes to ageing, seeking to resist it with campaigns of juvenilization.[1] And from this backward-facing perspective, unable to see where we are going, whatever plans and projects we come up with appear fraught with uncertainty. This comes from our inability to face both ways at once. If only we could be more certain, if only we knew what fate awaits us, then we could plan ahead with more confidence, prepare ourselves, perhaps even change things to weed out aspects of the future we don't like, and choose those we do. We could subject the future to a kind of artificial selection.

In pining for certainty, however, we should perhaps be careful what we wish for. For if there is one apparent certainty in life, it is that every one of us will eventually die. Even transhumanists, who dream that their present generation will be the last, are compelled to concede to the finitude of their own existence, prompting more extreme and wealthy believers to embark upon bizarre experiments in cryonic self-preservation in the hopes that they might be melted back into life once the problem of mortality has been finally cracked. Fading members of Generation Now, already past their prime and sliding down the far side of the bell-curve, will more likely reconcile themselves to the thought that even though death comes to everyone, at least they will die in the knowledge that generations will follow, facing uncertainties just as they did. There is hope in this, for whereas certainty augurs the dead-end, uncertainty opens up the field for life to carry on. It is, after all, a defining property of life that it always overreaches itself – that, far from running from beginning to end, every ending in life issues into new beginning. It is pure excess.

The curse of uncertainty is to present this excess as a deficit. To say that the future is uncertain is to suggest that life is not yet fully destined, that there is still work to be done to determine where it will finally lead. The word conveys a sense of incompletion, of unfinished business, of having not yet gained the full measure of the world that would yield to total predictive confidence. There are still gaps in our knowledge, missing pieces that remain to be inserted. To complete the picture, we typically look to what we call 'the Science'. This should not of course be confused with what practising scientists actually do. Indeed, scientists would be among the first to protest that they can never be certain about anything. Rather, the Science is an institutional apparatus, founded in ritual and rhetoric, the very *raison d'être* of which is to make up the deficit, to close the gap between uncertainty and certainty, allowing the frontrunners of Generation Now to project the future with a degree of confidence. And if the Science's predictions look grim, as they do today, it can propose mitigations to avoid complete catastrophe.

Yet not even the Science can admit to a future beyond the predictive horizons of the present. That, perhaps, is why today's younger generations are inclined to see the future less as a landscape extending indefinitely into the distance, than as a plateau bearing down upon them. The closer it gets, the more the tension ramps up, rising eventually to fever pitch. No previous generations have been so starkly presented with the prospect of the end of history.[2] To those about to take on the mantle of Generation Now, the future seems all too certain. There are doubters, of course, who would seek relief in denial, questioning the Science's authority and shrouding its forecasts in a pall of uncertainty. Yet no prediction comes without its estimate of risk, leaving assenters and doubters alike trapped in a language of probability, framed by an opposition between chance and necessity, which cannot countenance the creative impulse of a life that always exceeds itself. In the light of excess, however, what the deficit model presents as uncertainty takes on a quite different character. For then, *uncertainty reappears as possibility*. Far from plugging the breach of uncertainty, possibility surges right through it.[3]

Doing in undergoing

What would it take, then, to face the future as a realm not of uncertainty but of possibility? Today's young people, with their lives ahead of them, are often encouraged to think of the life course as a process of 'fulfilling their potential', that is, as a movement of progressive closure, in which all possible paths are gradually narrowed down to the one actually taken – which itself, at life's end, reaches its ultimate conclusion. As the anthropologist Clifford Geertz put it, in a now classic formulation, 'one of the most significant facts about us may finally be that we all begin with the natural equipment to live a thousand kinds of life but end in the end having lived only one'.[4] With one's potential fulfilled, there is nowhere further to go. That's it; life's up. But what if, instead of heading towards projected destinations, we were to push on from places already reached, along a path of renewal that knows no end? And what if, in doing so, we could continually recharge our potential? Could this be what the Pintupi, an Aboriginal people of Western Australia, meant when they told their ethnographer, Fred Myers, that life is a 'one-possibility thing'?[5]

For the Pintupi, the contours of life are those of the country in which they dwell, a country created by the ancestral beings as they moved around in the formative era known as the Dreaming. This era was not in the past, as modern people would understand it, nor is it a projection for the future. Its temporality is rather that of existence itself, an 'everywhen' whence every living thing comes into being for its allotted span. The Dreaming is pure possibility. Thus, every actual creature, as the incarnation of the ancestral power from which its vitality is derived, effectively finds itself on the inside of an eternal moment of world-creation. And where the ancestors led, life is bound to follow. This is the Law. Far from placing a lid on life, the Law lays down the conditions for its perpetual renewal, imparting an anarchival sense of direction. 'We have to sit down alongside of that Law', men say, 'like all the dead people who went before us'.[6] The dead are always ahead, yet ever present and active in the landscape. It is for the living to walk in their tracks. Pintupi people never cease to long for their ancestors.[7]

This is not, however, a movement from a starting-point to a destination. Instead, it carries on. Life is a one-possibility thing, in Pintupi eyes, because possibility *can only ever be one*. The idea that people could initially be presented with multiple possibilities, like a menu of options from which to choose, only for that menu to be narrowed as life proceeds, would make no sense to them. Theirs is not a world of opportunity, offering choices at every turn. Opportunities can be seized by those who have already pivoted on the present, and who see in them chances of future fulfilment. Every seizure is a hold-up that momentarily arrests, or even seeks to reverse, the renewal of the world. That's why it is eventually bound to run out of steam. But for those who follow the Dreaming, the world is a limitless source of vitality. Pintupi people, as they roam their desert landscape, are not fulfilling their potential but ever replenishing it. They may indeed become all the more powerful with advancing age. Yet even they have to take their chances, for example in decisions about where to go to find food and water. Life depends on getting them right.

How, then, can we best articulate chance and possibility? A possible answer can be found in the pragmatism of philosopher John Dewey.[8] In life, Dewey acknowledged, we do all kinds of things. We do first this, and then that, and as with this and that, there is a degree of certainty in the ends to be achieved. Yes, we know what we are doing! Every deed is an intentional act, like shooting an arrow at a target. We might miss, but we'll chance it nonetheless. Yet in everything we do, there is an experience we undergo. We are modified in body and mind, perhaps even transformed, by the doing of it. And the question, for Dewey, was to figure out the relation between the two – between the doing and the undergoing.[9] Do we put undergoing inside doing, sandwiched between the original intention and its final consummation? Is undergoing something that happens to us inside the act? If undergoing were thus contained within doing – or, as we would say, if possibility were encompassed within chance – then, Dewey reasoned, there could be no continuity from one deed to the next. Life would fragment into a scatter of disconnected episodes.

Yet this is not what happens in reality. Our experience, to the contrary, is that undergoing always *overflows* doing. Thanks to this overflow, whatever you do now takes into itself something of the experience of what you did before, and is in turn carried over into what you do next. With every doing, as Dewey put it, you are 'a somewhat different person'.[10] In short, undergoing lies precisely in the *excess* by which life overtakes the destinations thrown up in its wake. Let us describe every chance we take, as shown in Figure 4.1, by a transverse connection between an intention (I) and an objective (O). The life of undergoing still carries on, but in a direction orthogonal to these transverse links. In the figure, this is represented by the wavy line (P). Here, P stands for possibility. Opportunity cuts across, but life, as a 'one-possibility thing', is longitudinal. A life tracked along this line continually overtakes itself, yielding up not to objective consequences – for these are but discards along the way – but to further possibility, not just for itself but for all other lives with which it tangles, including, as we shall see, its generational offspring.

55

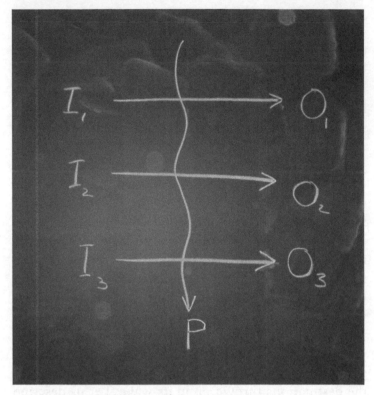

4.1 Opportunity and possibility

The structure of attention

Crucially, while every transverse connection denotes a line of intention, the longitudinal trail of possibility is a line of *attention*. Now there are two sides to attention: exposure and attunement. I take the idea of attunement from the ecological approach to perception pioneered by psychologist James Gibson.[11] For Gibson, perception is about noticing things in our surroundings that may help or hinder in the furtherance of our own activity. In a word, it is about picking up information that specifies what these things *afford*. And it can be learned. 'One can keep on learning to perceive', Gibson writes, 'for as long as life goes on'. In the practice of a craft, for example, skill lies in becoming sensitized to subtle variations in the material that a novice might miss. The carpenter attends to the grain of the wood, the smith to the ductility of iron. The skilled practitioner's perceptual system, in Gibson's terms, becomes 'attuned to information of a certain sort'. Yet, in this, the momentum is entirely on the side of the perceiver. It is as if the things to be perceived were already there, laid out in the environment, merely awaiting the practitioner's attention.

But what if everything is not already there? The world, after all, is not set in stone, but restless and fluid. Think of the fluxes of the weather, the ever-changing skies, the turn of the tides, the run of the river, the movements of animals and the growth of plants. Immersed in these fluxes, it is the perceiver who must wait upon the world, attending to it in the sense of abiding with it and doing its bidding. This is attention on the side of exposure. As philosopher of education Jan Masschelein explains, exposure (from the Latin *ex-positio*) literally means to be pulled out of position. To be or become attentive, Masschelein writes, 'is to expose oneself'.[12] In this condition, one can no longer take anything for granted. The sense of understanding – of having solid ground beneath one's feet – is shaken, leaving one vulnerable and hyperalert, wide-eyed in astonishment rather than narrowly focused on a target. For Masschelein, it is precisely in these moments of exposure that education occurs.[13] It is not so much an understanding as an undergoing, that strips away the veneer of certainty which offers an illusion of comfort and security, and opens to pure possibility.

Yet, if there are two sides to attention – of exposure and attunement, of waiting on the world and tuning to a world-in-waiting – then what is the relation between them? Surely, to embark on any activity means placing one's existence on the line. The safe course would be to stay put. No one can live like that, however. To live, we have to get moving, to push the boat out into the current of a world-in-formation. Thus, all undergoing begins in exposure. But as it proceeds, skills of perception and action, born of practice and experience, begin to kick in. We can see this in the most ubiquitous of human activities – namely, bipedal walking. Every step brings a moment of jeopardy. Falling forwards on one foot, you tumble into the void, only to regain your balance as the other foot comes to land on the ground ahead. Here, the bodily skill of footwork comes to the rescue, just before it is too late. What begins in the vulnerability of exposure ends in the mastery of attunement, providing in turn the ground from which the walker can once again submit to the hazard of exposure, in an alternation that can carry on forever.

This alternation, I believe, is fundamental to life. But just as life is a one-possibility thing, it is also unidirectional. That is, *submission leads and mastery follows* – never the reverse.[14] Where submission casts off into a world in becoming, setting us loose to fall, mastery restores our grip so we can keep going. The first is a moment of aspiration; the second, a moment of prehension. Out in front, an aspirant anticipation feels its way forward, improvising a passage through an as yet unformed world, while bringing up the rear is a pre-

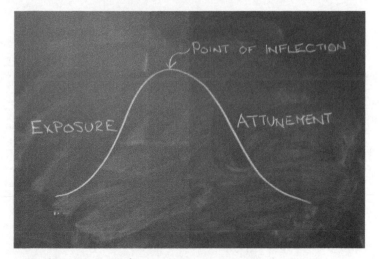

4.2 The structure of attention

hensile perception already accustomed to the ways of the world and skilled in observing and responding to its affordances. And as submission gives way to mastery, aspiration to prehension, anticipation to perception, and exposure to attunement, there is a moment of inflection. Here I return to the philosophy of Erin Manning, for whom inflection is not a movement in itself but a variation in the way movement moves, coming at the point where a tentative opening matures, from within 'the cleave of the event', into a firm sense of direction.[15] It marks the turn from undergoing into doing, as shown in Figure 4.2, whereupon the line of possibility discloses distinct and realizable opportunities.

In the foregoing, I have introduced two terms, 'aspiration' and 'anticipation', which we have not met before. Both require a bit of explanation. Literally, to aspire is to draw breath. It is an active, animated 'taking in'. And to take in, as Dewey observes, 'we must summon energy and pitch it in a responsive key'.[16] With this summoning and pitching, aspiration draws upon the animate powers of the lifeworld so as to cast them forth along a path of attention. Brimming with as yet undirected potential, with possibility, aspiration anticipates the future, but does not predict it. Prediction, as we've seen, belongs to the logic of certainty and uncertainty. Depending on the level of certainty, things may be predicted with greater or lesser confidence, or judged more or less probable. But anticipation belongs to the register of possibility. It is the temporal overshoot of a life that always wants to run ahead of itself. To anticipate is to open a path and improvise a passage. It is about foretelling more than projection, seeing into the future more than fixing an end point in the present, looking where you are going more than fixing your eyes on a target destination.

Surprise and astonishment

All life, then, is held in tension between submission and mastery, aspiration and prehension, anticipation and perception, exposure and attunement. In every case, the first leads, and the second follows. What leads is an *aspiration that wells up in attention.* What follows is a *precisely directed and skilfully executed manoeuvre.* As a one-possibility thing, moreover, this life begins nowhere, and ends nowhere, but carries on for all time – for the 'everywhen' of Australian Aboriginal cosmology. Yet we know that every mortal being will certainly die. How, then, can the infinitude of life be reconciled with the finitude of individual life cycles? With this, we return to the question of generations. We have already observed that life, as a one-possibility thing, is lived not transversally but longitudinally. Reprising our earlier analogy of the rope, this allows generations to overlap, and to forge a future in their collaboration. Each generation, as it begets the next, leans over its progeny in a gesture of care, even of love. Herein, surely, lies the true possibility of life. It is also why life is so astonishing. But, just as we have distinguished anticipation from prediction, so astonishment is not quite the same as surprise.

Prediction rests on the conceit that the world can be held to account. This is the way of science, and it is full of surprises. Scientists are surprised when their predictions turn out to be wrong. Yet they cherish the unexpected, since it shows that events are taking place and that progress is being made. According to the procedure of conjecture and refutation that science owes to the philosophy of Karl Popper,[17] advance in any field of inquiry lies in its cumulative record of predictive failures. Every conjecture is a hold-up, and is inevitably followed by its refutation as it collides with a world evolving in the reverse direction. This is the very obverse of longing. Things we long for, as we've seen, are always beyond reach. The way of longing is thus a way beyond, literally a *method* (from Classical Greek *meta*, 'beyond', plus *hodos*, 'way'). Science, to the contrary, prefers to target its objects head on, aiming not just to reach them but to grasp them within the categories of thought. It does so by means of protocols expressly devised to immunize the investigator from any affective contact with the phenomena under investigation. This is not method but methodology.

But where uncertainty breeds surprise, possibility makes way for astonishment. Those who long for the persons and things that captivate their attention –

including many so-called indigenous peoples, as well as most children whose minds are yet to be crushed by adult disciplinary oppression, along with old people who have thrown off its yoke – are perpetually astonished, but never surprised. They are not so arrogant as to believe that the world is predictable, even in principle, or that it can be held to account. Their openness, or exposure, renders them vulnerable, but it is also a source of strength, resilience and wisdom. It allows for ongoing responsiveness. An astonished attention is one that goes along with and answers to the movements of things. It allows us to *correspond* with them. By this I mean a process in which beings or things literally answer to one another as they go along together, facing in the *same* direction – for example, in the exchange of letters or words in conversation, or of gifts, or even in holding hands.[18] Correspondence, in this sense, is a joining *with* rather than a joining *up*. And that, precisely, is how entwined generations go along together: they correspond.

I recently heard a famous astronaut on the radio. He was excited about plans to establish a manned station on the moon, as a stepping stone to further exploration, first to Mars and then . . . who knows? Pushing out into ever-expanding frontiers, he believed, is what 'humanity is all about'. The astronaut was keen to inspire coming generations, to ignite their enthusiasm for the immense opportunities that await the human conquest of space. Doubtless he was sincere in his views. They put me in mind, however of an incident from my own childhood. I must have been 8 or 9 years old, and was walking home from school along a familiar path, with bushes on one side and fields on the other. From the bushes, I saw a rod-like object poking out. Was it the barrel of a gun?

Frightened, I crept forward, only to discover an old, bearded gentleman crouched in the undergrowth. The object was a telescope. 'What are you doing?' I asked. 'I'm looking at the moon', he replied. Might we look to the old man's example to recover the astonishment that today's science has crushed beneath the heavy boots of astronautical ambition?

Science is on a mission to reach the planets, and will fire as many rockets as it needs to complete it. But the old man had no such intention. His instrument proved, after all, not to be a gun. In his observation, he was not shooting a line into space, with his eye at one end and the moon at the other, but rather joining the arc of his attention, in real time, with the moon's radiance. As we see from Figure 4.3, this arc follows a line orthogonal

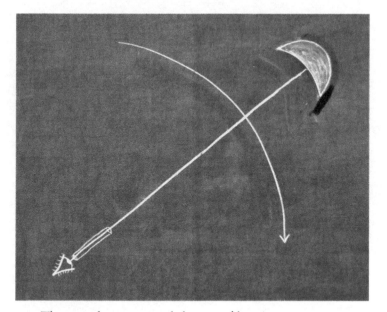

4.3 The eye, the moon and the arc of longing

to the line connecting the moon and the eye. It is an arc of longing. Should our aim, then, be to target the moon or to long for it? As a distinguished spokesman for Generation Now, the astronaut contemplates outer space as an unfinished project, and urges the young to sign up for it. But as the old man gently let me take a look, I felt an unforgettable sense of possibility. 'Bereft of knowledge before the heavens of my life', wrote the poet Rainer Maria Rilke, 'I stand astonished . . . I will yearn for no closer connections.'[19] Was it Rilke's double I met on my way home from school that day?

5

Loss and Extinction

The catalogue of species

The planet is on red alert, with warnings from the Science that a sixth mass extinction is not just imminent, but already upon us. There is nothing out of the ordinary, of course, in species going extinct; it is a fate that has awaited the overwhelming majority of species that have ever existed. What distinguishes mass extinction events is the sheer number and diversity of species lost within a comparatively short time span. Previous events, dating from around 447, 378, 252, 199 and 66 million years ago, have been variously attributed to climatic change, volcanic activity or asteroid strikes. The world's biota, though heavily impacted, did nothing to cause them. The sixth event, however, is unique in having been brought about largely as a consequence of the activities not just of living organisms, but of a single species among them. Precisely when this event began is much debated. There is nevertheless no doubt that the spasm under way today is recent, and attributable to direct overexploitation of other species by humans, the violent destruction of their habitats, the consequent release of new pathogens and, above all, changes in climate due to the combustion of fossil fuels on an industrial scale.

It is not my intention to question the Science, or to downplay the scale of the threat that the sixth extinction poses to life on Earth. A planet with only a quarter of today's approximately 8 million species – as some studies suggest could materialize within the next three centuries – would be but a shadow of the one we currently inhabit. Compared to the baseline rate of extinction, of roughly one species per million per year, current rates are hundreds or even thousands of times higher. I do want to argue, however, that to measure life's flourishing, or conversely its decline, by counting numbers of species found or lost betrays an attitude to the natural world – peculiar to Generation Now – which is hardly conducive to the continuing coexistence of human beings with other forms of life. For in staking a claim to the present, Generation Now has turned its back not only on its human predecessors, but also on the generations of other beings together with whom – or with which – they used to carry on their lives. In effect, this turn on the present converts nature into an archive of the past, for which the future can lie only in conservation.

This archival approach to the natural world is already evident in its partition by species. Setting aside the many controversies that surround the term, it suffices to note that for modern biology, reshaped in the wake of the Darwinian revolution, the species is a population of individuals which, while not identical, are deemed to share a family resemblance on account of their common ancestry. For every individual, species identity is given from the off. It is not something that develops through life, nor can it ever be changed or discarded. It is determined solely by a suite of attributes copied across from the previous generation, by inheritance, independently and in advance of the organism's life in the world: of the things it does, the places it inhabits, the relations it forms and the offspring it bears. Thus, the taxonomic grouping of individuals of a species on the basis of shared heritable attributes says nothing of their collective participation in a form of life. In line with the principles of the genealogical model on which it rests, species-thinking takes for granted that the life of the individual is expended in the episodic present, leaving only its attributional specifications for posterity.

But life goes on. In the words of poet Alastair Reid, it is all 'growing, flying, happening', inspiring in those who bear witness 'the *astonishment* of loving'.[1] Yet to partition the biosphere by species, and to count their number, is to siphon off the vitality both that animates every living creature and from which it is formed. It is to reduce each to a bundle of traits, which have only to be recognized and ticked off to assign it to its class. Sometimes, naturalists are *surprised* to come across an individual for which no class yet exists, yet the excess is immediately contained by proudly announcing the discovery of a new species. Another triumph for science; another surrender for life! It is as though the entire living world were a catalogue – otherwise known as 'biodiversity' – of which naturalists have appointed themselves as the curators. Each species is a catalogue entry; every individual organism a specimen of its type.

In the event that no further living specimens can be found, then science deems the species to be extinct. Consult the entry *Raphus cucullatus* (True Dodo) in the catalogue of nature, and it will return the null response, 'out of stock'.

Yet there can surely be no extinction without something to extinguish, some spark of vitality to put out. Where, then, is the spark in a species? Even as a creature is catalogued, and entered into the species archive, its vitality is quelled. The life is taken out of it. Thus, in its partition of the world, the science of biodiversity operates as an extinction machine which works at every turn to suppress the anarchival power of nature to bring forth, to beget. Is it not from this very power that nature takes its name? It comes from the Latin *natus*, 'to be born'. In his prose-poem *De rerum natura*, the Roman author Titus Lucretius Carus addressed nature, pointedly in the feminine, as 'the creatress of things' (*rerum natura creatrix*).[2] She was the begetter, the unearther. The paradox is that, in pivoting on the present, Generation Now has turned a nature that was once before us, ever birthing new life, into a nature behind us, to be preserved as heritage. This is to rob nature of the very promise of natality wherein its true essence lies. We may lament the loss of species, but the life is already lost, extinguished by the Science itself.[3]

Lineages of begetting

Can there, then, be such a thing as species-life? It would seem not, if my argument in the foregoing paragraphs is to be believed. For, as we've seen, the very logic of the genealogical model, which sets up species as objects of evolutionary change, also annuls all manifestations of life beyond the generational span of individual ontogenesis. In an essay dating from 1951, George Gaylord Simpson – one of the principal architects of the modern synthesis of evolutionary biology – defined the species thus: 'a phyletic lineage (ancestral-descendent sequence of interbreeding populations) evolving independently of others, with its own separate and unitary evolutionary role and tendencies'.[4] Simpson was a palaeontologist by trade, most at home in the museum of natural history. We can picture him at work, meticulously measuring up his fossil specimens with a view to lining them up in their correct ancestor–descendant sequences, on the basis of putatively inherited morphological variations. He is constructing the phylogenetic tree with its many branches, each representing what he calls a lineage. Where he sees extinction, it is at the terminus of a branch. But, unlike with the living tree, the branches of the lineage don't grow; rather, each is a chain of connections.

That's not the only way to imagine the species, however. There is another way, perhaps of more ancient provenance, which pre-empts the strictures of the genealogical model. 'Species', after all, comes from the Latin *specĕre*, 'to look, to behold'. Let us then open our eyes to the 'growing, flying, happening' – to recall Reid's words – that is going on all around us. What we see, in every instance, is not a specimen of a particular class of living things, or of things that once lived, but the manifestation of a certain way of being alive, of nature's revealing her hand in the unceasing work of creation, *natura naturans*. In this world, every creature is what it does: the woodpecker pecks wood, the anteater eats ants, the honeysuckle tenders its nectar to the suckling bee. To observe any creature is to witness this activity going on. It was in this sense that Karl Marx, in his *Economic and Political Manuscripts of 1844*, spoke of the animal's species-life. 'The whole character of a species', Marx asserted, 'is contained in the character of its life activity . . . *It is life-engendering life.*'[5] Every species, in a word, is a modality of begetting.

Marx was concerned to understand the switch of perspective from species-*life* to species-*being*. By the latter, he meant a stance, unique to humanity, which sets itself over and against nature, turning its back on her life-engendering powers, whereupon the lives and labours not only of human beings and their predecessors, but also of all other creatures, are seen reflected in objectified form, as if in a rear-view mirror. In this reflection, the productive activity of begetting reappears as the succession of its products, receding ever farther into the past. That is exactly what leads to the idea of the lineage as an ancestor–descendant sequence, of which Simpson's definition of the species offers an exemplary instance. But the lineage of begetting, as we found in Chapter 1, is of an entirely different order. It is a life of many lives, laid not transversally but longitudinally, in order of begetting and being begotten, and carried on in the collaboration of their overlap. Its lines don't connect but grow, branching and sprouting like those of the living tree. They are lines not of inheritance but of perdurance. What then does it mean for the lineage of begetting, of species-life, to go extinct?

So long as their intergenerational continuation is assured, different species will carry on their lives alongside one another, entangled in often complex webs of mutual dependency, and responding all the while to variations in each other's behaviour. Thom van Dooren, a leading voice in the emerging field of extinction studies, calls these species-lives *flight ways*, 'lines of intergenerational movement through deep history'.[6] A species-life is extinguished when, due to some more or less violent interruption to the collective labours of begetting, ageing and death no longer augur the possibility of renewal. What is lost is not the last remaining token of a type – it is, after all, perfectly possible for living specimens, artificially preserved, for example in a zoo, to outlast the broken ways of their forebears – but rather a mode of life, a tradition, along with the promise it holds for the future, not just for its own kind but for others as well. In the natural tangle of species-lives, it takes only one thread to be ruptured for the entire tangle to begin to unravel. This unravelling, however, far from being a one-off, dateable event like the demise of the last specimen, may be long drawn out.

Yet not even extinction studies have escaped the clutches of Generation Now, as this statement of intent from van Dooren reveals. He is interested, he says, in 'how we inherit ... the legacies of the past to shape possible futures'.[7] With this, species-life is promptly consigned to the archive, on the basis of which we of Generation Now can shape the future for our successors. Far from following in the wake of ancestral beings – be they human, other-than-human or spiritual – it is to turn our backs on them, converting their lives into a legacy to be conserved. The flight way turns out to be a line not of perdurance but of inheritance. To leave us in no doubt, van Dooren explicitly models genealogical succession as natural selection, working on the pool of inherited variation to fashion new forms of life. The one thing natural selection does *not* do, however, is to prolong the achievements of ancestors in the labours of descendants. For van Dooren to suggest otherwise shows how easy it is to slip from begetting to heredity.[8] This is a dangerous slip, and its consequences can be lethal, as we will see from the career of the concept of race.

Race and generation

'The race concept', anthropologist Eric Wolf reminds us, 'has presided over homicide and genocide.'[9] It has done so, however, only for as long as it has been tied to a certain understanding of human generations. Throughout history, indeed, the concepts of race and generation have been joined at the hip. One theory even posits an etymological link between the two terms, claiming that 'race' is derived from an abbreviation of the same Latin verb *generare*, 'to beget', which has also given us 'generation'. Whether true or not – another theory traces 'race' to Old French *haraz*, meaning a breeding enclosure for stud horses, from the Arabic *faras*, 'horse'[10] – ideas of race and generation have always been so closely bound that changing ways of thinking about one invariably have implications for thinking about the other as well. Thus, if generations are aligned longitudinally, then each race figures as a lineage of begetting, just one strand of the multitextured fabric of species-life. But when generations are stacked vertically, every race reappears as a particular layer or stratum of humanity, destined to supplant its predecessor and to be supplanted in its turn, along a phyletic lineage of species-heredity.

Early uses of the race-word are laden with connotations of kinship and shared ancestry, emphasizing the family pedigree, and often tinged with regret at the prospect of its eventual extinction, as in this line from playwright Thomas Shadwell's tragedy *The Libertine*, dating from 1676: 'I am the last of all my Family; my Race will fail, if I should fail.'[11] Generation turns to race, it seems, in times of strife, when the threads of species-life begin to unravel, imperilling the continuity of begetting. But what if this strife were itself considered the driver of progress? With this, the emphasis shifts from begetting to inheritance, in a history of intergenerational replacement which cuts across the flow of species-life rather than going along with it. 'In the never-ceasing wars of savages', wrote Charles Darwin in *The Descent of Man*, his attempt to apply the theory of natural selection to human evolution, 'successful tribes have supplanted other tribes', thanks to having a greater proportion among their number of 'well-endowed men'.[12] Progress inevitably follows, as the victors, blessed with superior powers of intellect and moral fortitude, bestow their endowments by inheritance on succeeding generations, only to be outdone by the next tribal cohort.

In this scenario, to borrow Darwin's words once again, 'extinction follows chiefly from the competition of tribe with tribe, and race with race'.[13] Here, as elsewhere, Darwin uses the words 'tribe' and 'race' interchangeably, such as when he anticipates a time, not long hence, when 'the civilised races of man will almost certainly exterminate, and replace, the savage races throughout the world'.[14] Just as any competition has winners and losers, progress and extinction figure in this account as two sides of the same coin. There cannot be one without the other. European colonial powers would go on to use Darwin's prognosis as a pretext to hasten the extermination of peoples indigenous to the lands they conquered, all in the name of civilizational advance. As late as the 1930s, Sir Arthur Keith – distinguished anatomist and one-time president of the Royal Anthropological Institute – would see in racial competition the very engine of evolutionary progress. Keith's colour-coded classification of the races of mankind ranged from black, through brown and yellow, to white. Mixing different colours, he said, would only lead to bland mediocrity. But if pure colours compete, lighter shades are bound to win, ultimately ridding the world of their darker cousins.[15]

How could such views have been entertained by men of education and high repute? Today, they strike us as both grotesque and repugnant. Yet we have no reason to doubt they were sincerely held. My point is that they were only thinkable within a paradigm of human generational history that attributes advance to a ratchet mechanism which notches up superior variations while consigning the inferior to eradication. Every present generation, in terms of this paradigm, is the site of an existential struggle for the future, which can only result in its eventual defeat, as its successor forcibly seizes the new present. Scientific raciology, of the kind embraced by the likes of Darwin and Keith, is best understood as a pathology of this paradigm, writ large. Only since we have come to think of human generations supplanting one another like layers in a stack, each of progressively superior stock, has the concept of race come to be freighted with the toxic connotations it has today. For Generation Now, this way of thinking not only feeds the transhumanist fantasy of final, death-defying victory in the struggle for existence; it also foments anxieties, popular among white supremacists, of an imminent 'great replacement'.

The doctrine of racial replacement is by no means confined, however, to the wilder shores of conspiracy theory. It continues even now to inform the science of human evolution, for example in the story it tells of how humans classified as Neanderthals (*Homo sapiens neanderthalensis*) were supplanted by those of the allegedly superior, 'anatomically modern' sub-species (*Homo sapiens sapiens*).[16] In a disturbing echo of the same story, it was long supposed that the Aboriginal people of Tasmania, once branded the most primitive on earth, were driven to extinction by white-skinned settlers in the nineteenth century. Yet there exists today a populous and vibrant Tasmanian Aboriginal community, all of whom number among their forebears not only Aboriginal people but also seal-hunters of European descent who had established relations with the island's indigenous inhabitants well before settlers arrived.[17] The story of the Tasmanians' extinction turns out to be a racist myth. Was it any different, then, in the Palaeolithic? All the evidence indicates that Neanderthals mingled with 'modern humans' over some fifty millennia. No more are humans of one sub-species or race today than they were of distinct sub-species in the past. They were mixed up then, as they still are now.

Conservation and conviviality

In short, mixed-up-ness is the way we humans are. Struggles for supremacy of one kind or colour over others have invariably given way, over the *longue durée* of history, to the improvisations of muddling along together. Every lineage knows that its best hope of securing its own continuity is to find other lineages to bind with. But to bind with others is also to differentiate one's own line from theirs. This is not the kind of difference, familiar to evolutionary theorists, that arises from the recombination, on successive generational levels, of hereditary particles of information – be they genetic or cultural – already broken off from the flow of life. I mean rather a difference that *emerges* as human generations, winding along together and rubbing shoulders with one another, continually enfold into their respective constitutions the qualities and dispositions of their coevals. This life of many lives, characterized by boundless difference rather than bounded diversity, abjures the divisions of any taxonomy. Nor is it confined to human beings. For not only do human lives unfold alongside a vast array of other manifestations of species-life, but these latter also may entwine with one another, even in the absence of any human activity.

What can extinction mean in a world in which every living being exists not as an object in itself, but as a knot in a tangle of life-lines? Does it make sense to speak of extinction at all? If lives cannot be contained, but run in and out of things like knotted threads, then nothing can truly go extinct unless everything does. Yet for any story of extinction to be told, others must remain to tell it. No creature can tell the story of its own extinction. If humans were to vanish from the face of the earth, would historians among the animals tell of their passing? More probably, they would carry on regardless, just as they did before humans first arrived. The animal, as Marx was keen to stress, 'is immediately one with its life activity'.[18] It may live its life as a story; we could even concede that, in living this life, it *tells* its story. What it cannot do, however, is to so differentiate the living from the telling as to weave stories of *other* lives into the living of its own, winding them together into a Story of many stories. This capacity is surely peculiar to human beings.

If that is so, then there can be no stories of extinction without humans to tell them. But this is not to say that extinction is a theme all human storytellers would recognize. My contention, to the contrary, is that extinction has only emerged as a theme alongside a certain reversal of temporal perspective associated with the rise of Generation Now, culminating today in what I call the Attenborough syndrome, named after the famed presenter of televised natural history programmes.[19] These hugely popular programmes beam spectacular images of species-life from every corner of the world into the living rooms of countless households, principally in the affluent global North. They come with the message that this world is a common heritage for all humanity, and that it is crying out for our protection. But there are normally no humans in the pictures. They appear only in supplements tacked on to the end of each episode, in which we see the filmmakers on location, often in the remotest of places, armed with their high-tech gear. Thus, packaged alongside the message that nature needs protection, is another – that salvation lies in the hands of a globetrotting technoscientific elite. How we envy them!

The idea is that the children of Generation Now, thrilled by what they see on screen, will dream of becoming scientists and filmmakers themselves, while the rest of us settle comfortably into our role as passive spectators of a natural world that exists only as a collection to be conserved. The rarity of the species depicted – its closeness to extinction – only heightens our excitement. Yet the technology that brings these images to our screens is the subject of another story, of industrial development. Perched on the fulcrum of the present, Generation Now finds itself faced with a choice between conservation and development, between protecting the heritage of the past and projecting a future that necessarily transcends it. Making space for both on a global surface of finite extent tends to pit one against the other, and the effort to find a resolution dominates the agenda of much current environmental policymaking on the international stage. The solution is commonly found in the rigid demarcation of protected areas, or 'parks', designated as havens for wildlife, free from human interference save for the activities of managers and researchers appointed to monitor species diversity and protect it as a legacy for coming generations.[20]

This has rarely turned out well for people indigenous to the lands affected, who have often found themselves barred from following their traditional ways by policies they played no part in shaping. For them, neither conservation nor development offers any assurance. Rather, the promise of the future lies in establishing lasting relations of conviviality, of *living together*, that allow creatures of different kinds to go their own ways, as their predecessors did, while nevertheless remaining attentive and responsive to each other's dispositions. In the stories indigenous people tell, species loss is attributed not to extinction but to a breach of convivial relations, due either to their own misdemeanours or to external impacts – not least, of the forcible imposition of policies of conservation or development considered disrespectful of creaturely ways. These policies effectively strip nature of its natality, its potential to beget, and hence its future. Biodiversity can only be preserved, locked into the divisions of the catalogue. There can be no conviviality unless and until we of Generation Now relinquish our claim to be the stakeholders of the present, and reorient our own lives in the *same* direction as those whose lives we affect to follow, into the future's past.

6

Recentring Anthropos

Humaning beyond humanity

In 1989, archaeologist Paul Mellars and palaeoan-
thropologist Chris Stringer published a jointly edited
compilation entitled *The Human Revolution*.[1] What
they were after was a turning point, without precedent
in the history of life, at which our earliest ancestors are
supposed to have put behind them the imperatives of
nature that all other creatures are destined to follow,
and embarked upon the path of ever-increasing invention, discovery and self-knowledge otherwise known
as culture or civilization. It was a search for the origins of what came to be known, rather enigmatically,
as 'anatomically modern humans'. We have already
encountered these characters in the previous chapter. Of similar build to the human beings of today,
and equipped with cognitive, linguistic and symbolic
faculties to match, they were nevertheless imagined
to be culturally at the starting block, as if gazing out
for the first time on the vast historical vistas that

their new-found faculties would reveal to them. While earlier, nominally 'archaic' human varieties, including Neanderthals, remained stuck in the past, merely following old ways, these 'modern' types had finally crossed an ontological threshold. Not merely human beings, they were finding out what it truly means to *be human*. They were the future.

That modern humans originated in a turnaround on nature was not, however, a discovery of twentieth-century science. It is rather a postulate on which the Science itself depends. Though Mellars, Stringer and their colleagues could draw on a fund of empirical data beyond anything available to their predecessors, the revolution they were after was already incorporated into a charter set down during the late seventeenth and eighteenth centuries by philosophers of the Enlightenment, convinced of the power of universal reason to emancipate humankind from earthly indigence. In their eyes, reason and nature pointed in opposite directions: nature to the past; reason to the future. Yet this left the human, irrefutably a creature of flesh and blood, with a foot in both, split between future and past, having to balance the fruits of civilization, including the Science, with a legacy of animal instincts. With this, the very word 'human' betokened a certain duplicity, epitomizing the dilemma of a creature torn between the two conditions and unable to decide to which it belongs. Is it a species of nature or a condition that transcends nature? Is science, in conferring the double-barrelled name *Homo sapiens sapiens* on the anatomically modern sub-species, trying to have it both ways?

Barely more than half a century ago, palaeoanthropologists could speak unflinchingly of the life and times

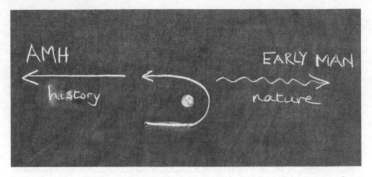

6.1 Early man, anatomically modern humans (AMH) and the 'human revolution'

of 'early man'.[2] Undeniably a *human being* by parentage, early man was deemed so far short of *being human* that his mode of existence had scarcely risen beyond that of his primate cousins, the great apes. It would require a U-turn of epic proportions, as indicated in Figure 6.1, for these ancient yet childlike humans finally to break with nature and launch their adventure into history. This breakthrough moment, enshrined in the founding myth of modernity, is recapitulated on the scale of a lifetime by every Generation Now as it comes of age. It is the point at which the threads of filiation – of begetting and being begotten – are cut, to be replaced by an assertive sense of self and its power to change the world. Thus does Generation Now stake its claim to the present. Like the age of early man in the human story, the 'early years' of childhood are consigned to the past; they are over. 'The past is a foreign country', wrote novelist L. P. Hartley in the opening words of his coming-of-age saga, *The Go-Between*: 'they do things differently there'.[3]

It is by way of its U-turn on the present – by putting nature behind and civilization in front – that

Generation Now nails its claim to essential humanity. This claim, however, is founded not on filiation
but on augmentation – the augmentation of nature by
reason, of the past by the future, of the old by the new.
Compared with other beings, the human is always 'more
than' or 'not merely'. Every creature begotten of man
and woman is, of course, human by descent, but in the
perspective of Generation Now, some are more human
than others: the adult more than the child, the scientist
or philosopher more than the early man of prehistory.
European colonists would use the same argument to justify the deportation, enslavement and even genocide of
the peoples whose lands they conquered, treating them
as less than human by comparison. For many contemporary critics, indeed, 'humanity' has become a word so
tainted by associations with racism and colonialism, so
duplicitous in its application, and so unjust in its consequences, that it would be better set aside. A world free
from colonial oppression, these critics argue, must also
be rid of humanity and its conceits.

It is one thing to call time on humanity, however; quite
another to do so on the human. As an Enlightenment
invention, 'humanity' is part of the legacy of the last few
centuries of European thought. But the word 'human' is
not. Its origins, though obscure, go back at least to classical Latin *humanus*, pertaining to persons, as opposed
to both animals and gods. Not that the ancient Romans
came with a clean sheet! They were the imperialists of
their age, and tended to reserve personhood for citizens,
while classing their human slaves with domestic animals. Doubtless in their time, as in ours, all manner of
abuse was inflicted – on animals, slaves and colonized
peoples – in the name of human civilization. Yet no

word deserves to be blamed for the abuses committed in its name. And there is no a priori reason why 'human' cannot be reclaimed for the process of species-life, of begetting and being begotten, by which generations carry on the collective work of self-creation. Why not turn 'human' into a verb, and call the process 'humaning'?[4] Humans would not then be more than beings of other kinds. Rather, in humaning, they would always be more than themselves.

The charge of exceptionalism

This suggestion is not new. On the contrary, it predates the Enlightenment by some four centuries. In his *Logica nova* of 1303, the Catalan mystic Ramon Llull defined the human in the following terms: *Homo est animal homificans*, 'The human is a humanifying animal.'[5] To humanify, in Llull's philosophy, is not to *humanize* the world, as Generation Now might see it, by imposing a preconceived design for the future upon the depositions of nature. It is rather for humans to forge their existence within the crucible of their common life. Humanness, then, is neither given from the start nor ever completed, but emerges as a productive achievement that generations, in their rope-like entwinement, have continually to work at for as long as life goes on. In this, of course, they are no different from other creatures. They, too, exist and persist – or, better, perdure – in the process of creating themselves and one another. This was the conclusion of philosopher Alfred North Whitehead, in his lectures of 1926 on *Religion in the Making*. There are not two things, the creativity and the creation. 'There is only one entity', Whitehead declared, 'the self-creating creature'.[6] No subjects or objects, then, only verbs.

The charge most often levelled against the claim of humanity is 'exceptionalism'. This, says the prosecution, comes from the habit of placing humans above and beyond every other form of life, at the apex of a pyramid that has the world at its feet. Having found humanity guilty as charged, the prosecution demands that the tables be turned, putting humans at the base and everything else on top. One of the effects of this inversion has been to rebrand what had formerly been called 'nonhumans' as 'more-than-humans'. This is a step in the right direction. Talk of nonhumans does nothing to counter toxic exceptionalism, but rather reinforces it, by smothering all those differences that make things and beings what they are under the blanket of what they are not. There is nothing to distinguish the woodpecker from the anteater or the honeysuckle; they are all the same in not being human, equally subject to human beck and call. More-than-human, however, reverses the order of precedence. Instead of we humans being more than them, they are now more than us. For the limit of nature, breached only by humans, it substitutes a limit of humanity, exceeded by beings of every other kind.

That the world we inhabit is home to more than only humans is obvious to anyone who has made a living from its lands and waters, though you might not believe it from the pronouncements of philosophers, broadly affiliated to what has come to be known as 'posthumanism', who have parroted their discovery of the 'more-than-human world' as though it were a breathtakingly new insight. This does not, however, make for a world of humans and more-than-humans.

Why should humans still be taken as the common denominator of all creation? If you were at home in the water, or in the sky, would you say of terrestrial creatures that they are more-than-fish, or more-than-bird? Are not fish and birds, just as much as humans, always more-than-themselves? As you will recall from Chapter 4, pure excess is a defining property of life. That's why I am not entirely in agreement with philosophers of post-humanism who see no human future beyond the limit of humanity. For them, a viable future can lie only *after* the human. My argument, to the contrary, is that for those prepared to follow in the ways of those who have gone before, the future lies in *humaning*.

It is surely only thus, by restoring their existence to an ever-worlding world, that humans to come will be enabled to play their part in future planetary flourishing. I make no apology, here, for proposing an explicitly *anthropocentric* vision of life on earth. By this, I mean a vision that places our anthropic selves at the heart of a world of experience which, for every one of us, radiates from where we are to embrace others of every possible variation and disposition, while acknowledging the debt we owe to these others for our own existence. This is far from how anthropocentrism is understood by the prosecution, for whom it is synonymous with exceptionalism. One could ask why an exceptionalist stance that elevates the human to the top of a pyramid should be accused of precisely the opposite – of positioning *Anthropos* at the world's very centre. Not only do such accusations mistake the apex for a centre. More seriously, the alternative they offer, of ecocentrism, also leaves no place for human life to enrich a world to come. Yet we know from archaeological studies that human activities, in foregoing times, have contributed massively to the abundance of life.[7] Why not again?

In the end, it all comes down to the direction of travel. The anthropocentrism that puts humankind at the apex stems from the arrogance of every Generation Now in thinking that it can halt the passage of time for its own projected ends. It cannot, of course, succeed in this, with the result that it will eventually capitulate to the next generational cohort, only for the latter to suffer the same fate, and so on. That's progress. And it leaves an accumulating pile of ruination in its wake. Remember the Angel of History? The Angel has turned his back to progress, yet the storm-blasts from Paradise prevent him from closing his wings. To follow the Angel's gaze, however, and to rejoin the ways of predecessors, facing in the same direction as they, is also to reposition human life from apex to centre, in amongst the generations that wind along together along paths of renewal that know no end. In this about-turn, humans do not cease to be exceptional. But the burden of exceptionality shifts from domination to coexistence. What creature besides the human, after all, can weave the stories of other lives with its own into a Story for the world?

Progress and sustainability

As we saw with race in the previous chapter, neither anthropocentrism nor exceptionalism is inherently toxic. Its toxicity is a product of the way we think of generations – namely, as stacking up. Imagining generations instead as winding along not only returns race to its original meaning as a lineage of begetting, but also restores humans from the apex to the centre, recognizing their exceptional responsibility for the flourishing of the life around them. This restoration is necessary, I believe, if we are to dig ourselves out from under the ruins of progress and find a way of living that is truly sustainable. For too long, as the earth's resources seemed inexhaustible, we have tried to hold on to both at once, marrying sustainability to the logic of progressive development by treating it as a matter of accounting, of balancing extraction against regrowth in a world still regarded as a standing reserve for the continuing benefit of a globally distributed humanity. Yet, for most people on the planet, who have access to neither corporate power nor the wealth that goes with it, the management of sustainability in this accounting sense has made it more difficult, not less, to inhabit the earth.

However, rather than dismissing the whole idea of sustainability as inherently tainted by corporate extractivism, a better and more hopeful course would be to revert to its origin in the idea of *keeping life going*. This is anthropocentric in the proper sense of placing human existence at the heart of a more-than-human world, from which emplaced centre we can renegotiate our relations with the earth and its inhabitants on a foundation of responsibility and care. To live sustainably in this sense means carrying on one's existence *with* others, responding to them as you go along, as they respond to you. Sustainability is correspondence. This is not a matter of finding the numerical balance of recruitment and loss, as so often supposed in the discourses of technoscience and environmental policymaking. It is rather about life cycles, about how living beings last or perdure, and about how they secure their own renewal. With this, all sorts of practices of everyday care, by which people look after family and kin, houses and fields, plants and animals, artefacts and landscapes, are accorded the value they deserve, as life-sustaining activities, instead of taking second place to the policy implementations of rational resource management.

A sustainability measured out in the longitudinal entwinement of generations, however, is fundamentally incompatible with the teleology of progressive development. They point in opposite directions. For one, a sustainable future lies in remembering ancestral ways, in longing; for the other, it lies in turning one's back on the ancestors so as to come face to face with a future on approach. The latter, of course, is the stance of Generation Now. In its sights, unsustainability – like mortality – represents a problem to be fixed. Wishing its generation to be the last, it dreams of engineering a total, self-regulating earth-system that would run itself in perpetuity. This dream, however, is as illusory as the transhumanist fantasy of solving death. In reality, the 'sustainable future' that Generation Now plans for evermore is just that: a plan, and, like all plans, it is destined to be replaced. Longing, by contrast, is an improvisation. It has no targets, no final goals, only an irrepressible desire to carry on. Recall, from Chapter 4, my story of the old man and the astronaut. The old man was longing for the moon, but the astronaut wanted a rocket that would take him there. Whose approach was the more sustainable?

Yet you will be bound to ask: how can renewal come from following old ways? Surely old and new are opposites, belonging respectively to the past and to the future. So they are, indeed, from the perspective of Generation Now, with its feet firmly planted in the present. There can be no future, it insists, without progress, and no progress without innovation. Is this not the source of the very augmentation that, historically, has lifted humanity from the slow lane of natural evolution into the fast track of culture and civilization? Since the novelty of things can be judged only by their departure from what has gone before, old things are bound to present themselves as repetitions. The appearance of every new thing is an event in chronological time, but in its subsequent repetition it becomes part of the beat of time itself. You can see this in the way Generation Now treats its old people. In their prime, when their generation was in charge, these people had indeed made history by adding to the accumulating stock of 'firsts'. But now, though we still celebrate their anniversaries, we don't expect them to *do* anything beyond recollecting old times.[8]

Novelty is one thing, however; renewal another. Robert Pogue Harrison, reflecting on the meaning of newness in the title of Vico's *New Science*, a work to which we referred in Chapter 3, observes that 'genuine newness entails the rejuvenation, rather than the repudiation, of that from which it seeks freedom and independence'. Without renewal, as Harrison wryly puts it, the new 'gets old in a hurry'. It is destined for the scrapheap.[9] Let me return to my earlier distinction between life as a 'one-possibility thing', and the multiple opportunities it throws up.[10] Every novelty is an opportunity seized, and ends with its realization. But renewal fills us with a sense of possibility, and of hope, as when, in springtime, the whole world bursts back into life, presaging a summer harvest. We can begin again! What affects us is the begetting, the relaying of the life process from season to season. And as every plant and animal is telling us, loud and clear, there is renewal only in following old trails. Remembering is the way to the future. While progress may lie in the accumulation of novelties thrown up en route, for sustainability what really counts is the continuity of life.

Of herds and turbines

Since time immemorial, the mountainous interior of northern Norway has been populated by herds of reindeer, which have provided the region's indigenous people, the Sámi, with their principal source of livelihood. The animals had formerly been hunted, but since the seventeenth century, as wild herds diminished, a regime of nomadic pastoralism emerged in its place. Over the years, the techniques and regulatory frameworks of herding, together with market conditions and everyday living arrangements, have altered a great deal. Behind these changes, however, the bond between people, reindeer and land has remained indissoluble. Herdsmen continue both to guide and to follow their animals, through a milieu suffused with the presence of ancestors. More recently, however, they have had to contend with competing demands to use the land – for example, for military training, mining and hydropower generation. Today, a new competitor has appeared in the form of batteries of wind turbines, constructed as part of a massive, state-sponsored programme of sustainable development to provide pollution-free renewable energy. The programme's promoters argue that the impact of this development on reindeer herding should be negligible. The animals are still free to roam and graze as before. But the herders themselves take a different view.

The sight and sound of the turbines, they protest, disturb the reindeer. This is in addition to the disruption caused during the initial phase of construction. Deer have long memories, and once deterred from visiting an area, they can be reluctant to return.[11] Behind these objections, however, lies a more fundamental clash between different orders of reality. One is the generative order of the living world; the other, the order of a world erected by human artifice upon the physical bedrock of nature. In the collision between these orders, represented by people and herds on the one hand, and turbines on the other, which has the upper hand? In the glare of the present, the turbines might appear to win out, shining symbols of the human conquest of nature, guided by reason and implemented through technical ingenuity. They are monuments to progress. But animals don't do progress, and have no place in the artificial order of the turbine. No sooner do we rejoin the herds, then, than the turbines fade like phantoms into the mist. Long after they have vanished, reindeer will still migrate, and people will follow, even as night follows day and the seasons continue to turn.

Both wind and time have different meanings here. Reindeer are as aerial as they are terrestrial, ever holding their noses to the breeze. In their perception, the milieu is not so much a landscape as a melange of air currents, set up through the wind's scouring the earth as it skirts the hills, funnels through valleys, or whips the trees.[12] But these aerial perturbations, which mean everything to the deer, mean nothing to the turbine. The wind may blow light or strong, from this direction or that, but to the turbine's blades it is merely a force of propulsion. Moreover, turbines never age. Standing tall, yet pinned to the ground at preassigned locations, these apotheoses of Generation Now straddle the landscape like an invading army of perfect clones. Their rotating blades, circling rather than winding, describe a time that repeats without passing. As if by magic, they bring time's passage to a halt, putting the world on pause. Every identical turbine tower literally stakes its claim to a never-ending present. But the world carries on regardless, taking with it only those things, such as living beings, capable of rejuvenation. Among them are reindeer, and the people who accompany them.

Not just wind and time, then. The two orders also have different relations to the earth. To mount a turbine, you have first to dig a pit and fill it with a thick layer of reinforced concrete. The sections of the turbine tower are then lifted into place from above, using a crane, which also lifts the preassembled blades unit into position on the axis of the nacelle, at the top of the tower. Thus, in the very principles of its construction, the turbine proclaims the absolute separation of earth and sky. That's why it is such a jarring presence in the milieu of reindeer herding, which is nothing if not the commingling of the two. Reindeer don't take chunks out of the earth to seal it against the sky, but nibble to meet their needs, leaving the rest untouched. The ground is for grazing. Yet its surface is indistinct, and seasonally variable, from winter's snow, through which deer have to dig to access the lichen cover beneath, to summer's mosaic of lush vegetation and waterlogged marsh, bare rock and desert sand. Where the ground lies, it is impossible to say, for it is all these things rolled into one.

And the people who live with herds? What is the earth to them? How should we describe their way of life? Words like 'landscape' and 'culture' are not perhaps the most appropriate. Carried along on the windswept surfaces of moor or snow, herdsmen are called upon to respond in their movements to ever varying conditions of the sky above and the earth below. These, more than the intervening landscape, command their attention. Could what we are used to calling the 'culture' of an indigenous people like the Sámi lie in precisely this – not an inheritance, ready and available to be passed on, whether inside people's heads or in the exterior landscape, but something more like an atmosphere, diffuse and unbounded, breathed by those who find themselves in its midst? It is at once a cosmic milieu, formed of the unison of earth and sky in which everything lives, and a field of affective relations, born of the intimacy of overlapping generations. This atmosphere cannot be transmitted like a package from one generation to the next. It can only be lived in their collaboration. And it is in the living that it is both produced and reproduced – or, in a word, *sustained*.

7

The Way of Education

The academic posture

Education is the way a society produces its future. But what kind of future is this? Is it one of replacement, enabling the young to take on the mantle of Generation Now, as the generation of their teachers goes into decline? Or is it one of perpetuation, bringing new people into the fold of a collective life in which all are embarked together? Does the teacher, having turned on the present, confront the class of the next generation face to face, in a posture of instruction, or does she continue along the ways of predecessors, beckoning her students to follow in a gesture of companionship? Do the students appear before her, or follow after? This is a good moment to revisit the contrast between the rope and the stack, as ways of thinking about generations and their passage. With the stack, every generation has its own layer, furnishing its members, as philosopher Immanuel Kant put it, with 'the ground on which [their] knowledge is acquired and applied'.[1] But with the rope there is no such ground; rather, each strand must find purchase in the world by binding with others. How does this contrast bear upon the nature and purpose of education?

For more than three centuries in the Western world, education has been regarded as the engine of social progress. It has been the means by which advances in human knowledge, forged by bringing powers of reason to bear upon the material of empirical observation, have been passed from one generation to the next, allowing each to stand on the shoulders of its predecessors. An education that conforms to this progressive principle naturally gives pride of place to subjects of study deemed by the standards of formal pedagogy to be *academic*. For, as a place of learning, the academy – be it a school, college or university – is founded on a claim to superior knowledge of how the world works, at least as compared with the knowledge of so-called lay practitioners, which, by contrast, is so tightly bound to experience as to remain out of reach of explication and analysis. Almost by definition, academic knowledge situates itself on a higher plane, at one remove from the messy theatres of practice in which it might be put to use, if at all. That's why academic study typically separates learning from doing, the transmission of knowledge between generations from its application within them.

I shall call the attitude of the teacher who stands to face her students the *academic posture*. It is premised on her social accreditation with both superior knowledge and the qualification to pass it on. The aim is to raise students from a presumed baseline of ignorance, through a series of stages, to an adult level of understanding, on which they can build when their time

comes. The effect of this posture, however, has been to push to the margins a range of subjects that appeal – as we might say in our modern idiom – more to sense than to reason, or to criteria of perfection more aesthetic than logical. It is not that these subjects, ranging from art and craft to music and dance, have no place in the curriculum. On the contrary – even in a society wedded to the ideal of progress, there is widespread recognition of the need to complement the detached objectivity, cold logic and analytic rigour of academic study with something more hands-on and subjective, more attuned to feeling, empathy and holistic understanding. An education in non-academic subjects, we are told, offers students a rounded formation that enhances their abilities to relate to their surroundings.

This complementarity of academic and non-academic subjects is deeply sedimented in the modern constitution, with its divisions between objective knowledge and subjective experience, and between reason and expression. Scientists even tell us that it is wired into the human brain, in its split between left and right hemispheres! The left is the seat of intellect, the right the seat of empathy; neither can function without the other. But I believe more is at stake here than complementarity. What truly distinguishes non-academic pedagogy, in my view, is a fundamental difference of posture – of companionship rather than confrontation. In this, teacher and students face in the same direction, the one *leaning over* the others. Education, then, is a joint undertaking, driven not by a humanistic ideal of progressive improvement but by a passion to seek the truth of what is real and present in the world. Far from opening up a space for the cultivation of subjective self-expression,

alongside and as a counterbalance to the space of objective knowledge transfer, this is to bring students into an ongoing dialogue with the world itself, guiding their attention towards things or beings to be found there, and exploring the conditions of coexistence with them.[2]

I call this kind of education *undercommoning*.[3] By this, I mean the very opposite of understanding, as configured by the academic posture. Understanding lays a ground of certain knowledge, literally a platform to stand on, furnishing in turn a secure foundation for future endeavours. With understanding, knowledge preempts attention. Why bother to attend, when you already know? Undercommoning, to the contrary, sweeps the rug from under our feet. Nothing is certain, but, by the same token, everything is possible. Having no solid base on which to build, whether singly or in association, compels us to bind with one another, like the strands of the rope, lest we are cast off. Undercommoning, then, is *a way of living together in possibility*, calling for the mutual attention and response that I have already introduced, in Chapter 4, as correspondence.[4] To correspond with other things or beings is not to fall back on what you have in common with them from the start, but to welcome them into your presence just as they are, to find ways to go along together with them and, in so doing, to fashion a community of relations. Therein lies the essence of the posture of companionship.

Reason and response-ability

Far from providing the curriculum with a complement of subjects peripheral to the academic core, I believe this posture of leaning over, laden with care and com-

passion, has the potential to transform the very purpose of education, across *every* field of study, from the efficient transmission of knowledge from teachers of one generation to students of the next, to opening a path, or showing the way, guiding attention towards aspects of the world that might repay further scrutiny. Literally, after all, 'to educate' means to 'lead out' (from the Latin *ex*, 'out', plus *ducere*, 'to lead'). Taken in this original sense, education leads us out into the world, so that we can both attend and respond to it. And, in leading out, it persistently pulls us away from established standpoints, from any claims we might make to the present. An education that leads out in front, however, also leans over behind. Even as the educator proceeds along the ways of predecessors, she also 'bends over backwards', as we say, to look after her student followers. Leading out is to leaning over, here, as ageing is to begetting.[5] One, as shown in Figure 7.1, is the inverse of the other.

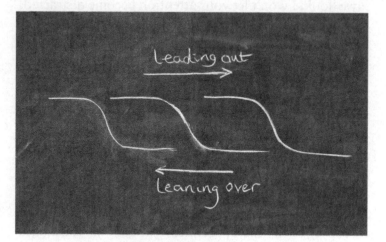

7.1 Leading out and leaning over

For Jan Masschelein, to whose philosophy of education I have already alluded,[6] this practice of leading out and leaning over amounts to what he calls 'poor pedagogy'. Such pedagogy has no position to uphold, no body of knowledge to transmit, no great project to realize. It works, rather, through the displacement of its disciples, through moving them out of position, or in a word, through *exposure*. Like taking a walk outside, in which every step is potentially hazardous but also offers an opening to the world, a poor pedagogy, according to Masschelein, invites us to relinquish our comfort zone for the discomforts of the road, exchanging strength and security for weakness and vulnerability. Far from arming us with knowledge, or shoring up our defences so we can better cope with adversity, the aim of poor pedagogy is to disarm, to expose, and by the same token to sharpen attention to the world around us, so that we can respond with skill and sensitivity to what is going on there. It is a pedagogy, in Masschelein's words, which says: 'look, I won't let your attention become distracted, look! Instead of waiting for thrills and a denouement, for stories and explanations, look!'[7]

In this undertaking of poor pedagogy, of leading out and leaning over, teachers and students go along in each other's company, fellow travellers in the undercommons. The journey can be difficult, risky and uncomfortable, with no guaranteed outcome. The job of the teacher is certainly not to make things easy for students. It is, however, to set an example, to serve as a generous guide, a constant companion and a tireless critic. And students, following their teacher's example, should not be afraid to copy, just as the apprentice will copy in learning a craft. There is no expectation on students to innovate, as

in the academic posture which measures added value in educational progression by the novelty of outcomes, and disqualifies copying as plagiarism. In the posture of companionship, copying is not plagiarism, it is practice. As an apprentice, the student practises under the eyes of the teacher, only, eventually, to become those eyes, watching in turn over the next generation. And so the tradition carries on, founded on the assurance that students, who cannot be *compelled* to learn, are nevertheless eager to join in the endeavours of their teachers, and to relay the torch of learning for generations to come.

An education in the undercommons thus calls for a readiness to go along with others, and to answer to them as you go. In a word, it fosters *response-ability*. This is not a new idea. So far as I know, it was first introduced by composer John Cage, in a lecture delivered in 1957. Only in the presence of things, Cage said, can we feel them, and only through feeling can we respond. Apparently unaware of this precedent, cultural theorist Donna Haraway has recently reinvented the term in much the same sense. Response-ability, she says, is a 'praxis of care and response'. Yet Cage's was not the only precedent, for a decade before Haraway latched on to the term it was also used by educational theorist Gert Biesta.[8] For Biesta, response-ability refers to a certain *voice*. It is a voice of one's own that nevertheless only comes forth in soliciting others to respond, in theirs. Like a line in a conversation, or in polyphonic singing, every voice continually emerges in and through its joining with, and differentiating from, the voices of others. What would it mean for education, Biesta asks, to prioritize the development of response-ability over the cultivation of reason?

The voice of reason belongs to no one. It transcends all variations of experience. It is this voice, both instructive and impersonal, that academic education aims to inculcate in students, specifically by dissociating knowledge from personal experience and making it accessible to all. In the community of reason, as philosopher Alphonso Lingis puts it, everyone is interchangeable. Problems have their right answers, which are the same whoever happens to come up with them. A mathematical theorem, for example, gives no hint of the life and times of the mathematician; a law of nature, or of society, speaks nothing of the scientists or jurists who legislate on its behalf. A pedagogy of response-ability, however, would reverse the priorities of the academic posture, positioning attention to ever-emergent difference ahead of standardized measures of attainment. If, in the community of reason, it doesn't matter who you are so long as it's new, in the community of response-ability, it matters more than anything. For it is precisely because every voice in the community is different that its people are bound together. It is a community, as Lingis says, 'of those who have nothing in common'.[9] Having nothing in common, each has something to give.

New people, old ways

Every human being, of course, is born into a world. This is the elementary fact of natality. It means that, for those who have already been around for a while, and are familiar with the ways of this world, their first task is to *introduce* these new beings into it. This, for political philosopher Hannah Arendt, is the task of education. It is a relation between adults and children, in which the former shoulder the responsibility for the latter's development. Throughout most of human history, as Arendt observes, this relation has arisen normally and naturally 'from the fact that people of all ages are always simultaneously together in the world'.[10] Thanks to intergenerational coexistence, as we saw in Chapter 2, young people have ample opportunity to hear the stories and practise the skills of their elders, and to relay them in the passage of their own lives, becoming exemplary practitioners and storytellers, in their turn, for generations to come. It is by lovingly leaning over along their old ways, as they lead out into the future, that elders create the conditions for the young to embark on a path of rejuvenation. In this lies the continuity of tradition.

Yet, in our present day and age, this continuity has been ruptured. Generations have been so prised apart that they no longer overlap but, rather, stack up. With the consequent breakdown of everyday intergenerational relations, elders are prevented from introducing young people into traditional lifeways, as they used to do. The responsibility for their education has been transferred, in large part, to the state. And for Arendt – writing in 1954, in the aftermath of the Second World War – it was the failure of the state to discharge the responsibility vested in it, by way of this transfer, that underlies what she saw as today's 'crisis in education'. Instead of introducing young people into an old world, the state sets out to prepare them for a new one, the order of which it has decreed by fiat. Such preparation, Arendt thinks, offers but a pretence of education, the real purpose of which is not to introduce the young but to indoctrinate them. The coercive effect of this indoctrination is to deny them any chance at making a future they can call their own, since by the time they arrive on the scene the tomorrow's world they were promised will already be yesterday's.

We can plainly recognize in this the attitude of Generation Now, which takes it upon itself to cast the future as a project even as it consigns the past to heritage. Its agents of education, seeing the next generation heading towards them and threatening eventually to usurp their pre-eminence, demand that young people conform to the new order while standing as gatekeepers, controlling the conditions of their admission to it. Yet for these young people, their only hope of making a mark, as a *new* generation, lies in repudiating the future predesigned for them, and projecting another in its place. The result is that stuttering series of generational replacements we call progress. But in this, echoing to the lament of the Angel of History, Arendt sees only ruination. Her face, like the Angel's, is resolutely turned towards traditional ways. These alone offer a viable path into the future. And the question of education, for Arendt, is whether our longing for this old world, our *amor mundi*, is sufficiently intense to enable us to carry the burden of introducing new lives into it. For only if it is can there be hope of renewal for generations to come.[11]

The burden is indeed a heavy one. It takes diligent work, on the part of both adults and children. Arendt's philosophy comes across as not just conservative in its commitment to tradition, but stern, austere and authoritarian. Not for her the laissez-faire approach of learning by doing. Education, she says, isn't just a matter of picking things up as you go along. While this might suffice for acquiring the 'art of living', the purpose of education is to teach children 'what the world is like'.[12] Things need to be explained. It is one thing, for example, for children to pick up their mother tongue, quite another to study its grammar and syntax. They won't do that by playing around! Children need to be taught by adults who know more than they do, and it is the responsibility of the latter to make sure this happens. Their qualification to teach lies in knowing more, but it is on their assumption of responsibility, not on what they know, that their authority rests. Anyone who refuses to take responsibility, Arendt declares, 'should not have children and must not be allowed to take part in educating them'.[13] No responsibility, no authority!

These are robust words. I doubt that Arendt, even in her darkest moments, would have wished for a world in which the right to beget is dictated by philosophers. What matters for us, however, is the meaning of authority. We tend to assume any exercise of authority is confrontational. As a subject, it is something you face. But Arendt's argument, as indicated in Figure 7.2, implies the quite different posture of leaning over. The authoritarian figure is a guardian, not a tyrant. This might be why Arendt is so keen to distinguish the authority that rests on responsibility from the qualification that rests on superior knowledge. The idea that the teacher should be qualified to explain what the world is like certainly smacks of the academic posture. It sets the knowledgeable adult over and against the ignorant child. But responsibility calls for care and protection. The responsible parent or teacher cherishes the child, much as the gardener nurtures a seedling in the ground, creating a sheltered milieu for them to grow. And there can be no responsibility without response-ability, without

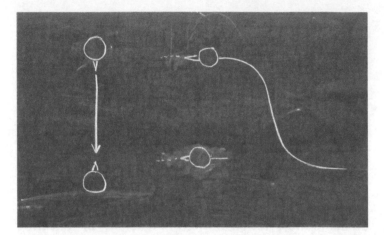

7.2 Authority as confrontation (left) and as the exercise of responsibility (right)

the voice of the one, who leans or watches over, soliciting the voice of the other with which it corresponds.

Wisdom and curiosity

If responsible education needs a place of shelter, what then is it to be shielded from? Not the manifold of earth and sky, home to living beings, which furnishes the wherewithal for growth, but the onslaught of the new that every Generation Now, having captured the public and political domain, inflicts upon it. In Arendt's vision, these two worlds – one dedicated to the renewal of life, the other to the fabrication of society – are implacably opposed. Life 'emerges from darkness', but is ever at risk of being overwhelmed by 'the merciless glare of the public realm'.[14] The fact that education is now in crisis, she thinks, is due to the loss of security that leaves students at the mercy of a system of public schooling which has no other objective than to indoctrinate them into a future of its own making. But could it be otherwise? Can we envision a society in which the little space of shelter, of leaning over, rather than having to shield itself from the public gaze, could serve as a beacon of social regeneration? What if the generations of young and old, after their increasingly painful institutional segregation, could resume their co-participation in the labours of begetting?

These questions, I believe, have massive implications for the way we think about education, about the young and the elderly, and about the potential of their collaboration. Today's parents are naturally keen that their children should do well in the world, and so the education they want for them is both rich and strong: rich in its knowledge content, strong in the power and confidence it bestows. Mainstream academic education strives to satisfy these demands. It speaks with the voice of reason, pitting adult knowledge against childhood ignorance. It confers rank on its recipients, upping their life-chances in a competitive society. Knowledge is one thing, however; wisdom, quite another. Indeed, there is wisdom in *not-knowing*. If to know is to accommodate worldly matters within the compartments of thought, to be wise is to throw open the doors of perception, to let the world in upon the field of attention and deliberation. It is to welcome others into our presence, not to overpower them or to beat them off. It is to watch and listen, and to learn. If knowledge arms us against adversaries, wisdom disarms. But, by the same token, it leaves us exposed and vulnerable.

This is the vulnerability of elders, induced not just by physical debilitation, but by the dawning realization,

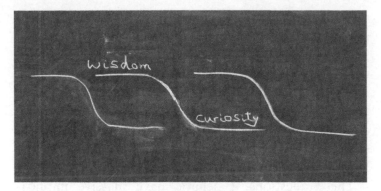

7.3 The voices of wisdom and curiosity

from lifelong experience, of how little they know. For them, knowledge is tempered by humility. And among the young who come under their elders' wings, wisdom feeds curiosity. Children are curious because their attention is open and alert, not yet stopped up by the academic education that Generation Now is waiting to inflict upon them. Might grandparents prefer this awakening of curiosity for their grandchildren? A pedagogy that joins these alternate generations in the companionable posture of leading out and leaning over, as shown in Figure 7.3, would bring voices other than that of reason into the conversation: the voices of wisdom, among the elderly, and of curiosity, among the young, each soliciting the other in a correspondence aligned with the temporal stretch of longing. Where reason speaks with words of order, stopping recipients in their tracks, wisdom and curiosity speak with words of passage, opening to life.[15] The pedagogy they deliver may be poor, having little by way of readymade content to transmit, and weak in disarming the defences of both parties. But could there be strength in weakness, richness in poverty?

Neither juvenile curiosity nor seasoned wisdom, to be sure, hold much esteem in a society that values objective knowledge and the operations of reason above all else. Knowledge, putting answers before questions, stamps out curiosity; reason, privileging cognition over attention, truncates wisdom. Indeed, within the value system underlying mainstream institutions of education and social care, dedicated respectively to preparing children for a predetermined future and sequestering the elderly for whom it came too late, the innocence of curiosity is assessed as a deficiency of knowledge, and the humility of wisdom as a deficiency of reason – the former branded as ignorance, the latter as senility. For Generation Now, in command of the present, the idea that the senile and the ignorant might together forge the future would be manifestly absurd. To unite wisdom and curiosity, however, appears not merely prudent but necessary for the renewal of life for coming generations. This is neither a nostalgic hankering for a lost past, nor a utopian fantasy for the future, but a foundation for hope. To turn hope into reality, however, old and young have first to reconvene, turning their productive and mutually transformative collaboration into a force of renewal for the common good.[16]

We have arrived, finally, at an alternative model of education. Its passion is *amor mundi*, love for the world, or what we have called longing, and its vocation is not to bring the young into the light, but *to teach them to see in the dark* – 'the dark of the living past where the future's possibilities call out across time for retrieval'.[17] Instead of proposing a complementarity of academic and non-academic subjects, our model places the posture of leading out and leaning over before any disciplinary divisions of academic standing. A subject like mathematics, for example, often placed at the pinnacle of academic genius, draws upon a depth of ancestral wisdom as profound as that of any craft. Nor is learning a craft any less challenging intellectually than studying mathematics.[18] In the companionship of the undercommons, subjects are not ranked on a ladder of attainment by the divisions of a formal curriculum, but retrieved and renewed in the voices of those who study them. As they wind around one another, these voices weave a rope of many strands that carries on as life does, never farther from an origin or closer to an end. This rope is the way of education.

8

After Science and Technology

From STEM to STEAM

Generation Now and the Science depend upon each other. Generation Now needs the Science to close the deficit of uncertainty in its forecasts for the future; the Science needs Generation Now for the institutional support to maintain its costly infrastructure of laboratories, research stations and computational machines, along with the experts to operate them. Since the turn of the millennium, however, the Science has increasingly sailed under another flag – namely, STEM. Standing for 'science, technology, engineering and mathematics', STEM is an acronym. There is a reason why Generation Now has a penchant for acronyms, which pepper its language of policy and practice in fields ranging from commerce to defence. For they allow us to speak or write of things without naming them. We already saw, in Chapter 1,[1] how pronouncing the names of persons, in a genealogical recitation, is part of the process of introducing their lives into lineages of begetting. It is the same with things.

To name them is to call them up, to dwell on them and to join our lives with theirs. But this is precisely what Generation Now, in its appeal to reason, wants to avoid. With the acronym, it can bypass response-ability.

This argument applies equally to the naming of fields of study, or what are often called disciplines. These names matter. Spelled out in full, they carry the weight of tradition, and are bound up with the lives and identities of their practitioners. If, for example, I were to declare that 'I am a philosopher', I would be saying something about myself, and about how my own ways of thinking and feeling have been shaped by the scholars with whom, and the works with which, I have studied. I would profess, quite literally, to a love of wisdom and learning, founded in an attitude of curiosity, responsiveness and care.[2] I do not believe it is any different in practice for disciplines that nowadays come under the umbrella of science. It is there in the biologist's attention to living things, in the chemist's attention to the properties of materials, in the physicist's attention to matter itself. Technology and engineering, likewise, resemble craft in the perceptual acuity and respect for materials required of their practitioners. As for mathematics, its rootedness in gesture, rhythm and trace have been evident since antiquity, notwithstanding the myths of intellectual genius that have grown up around it.

Breathe the word 'science', 'technology', 'engineering' or 'mathematics', not casually but with deliberation, pause on it for a while, and you are transported into a landscape of inquiry, stretching as far as the eye can see, and beyond, along paths already trodden by illustrious predecessors. Every discipline so named is a lineage of begetting, wound like a rope from the overlapping scholarly lives of its numerous practitioners. And, as a student, your task is to carry it on. The acronym STEM, however, cuts like a knife through these several lineages. In its enunciation, it conveys no trace of affect. Bypassing the names of disciplines, the acronym also bypasses any feeling we might have for them. It rouses no passions, no memories, no sense of longing. It betokens nothing but sterile, detached instrumentality. Substituting acronyms for the traditional names of disciplines, therefore, is not just a simple matter of expository convenience. It is, rather, an index of their wholesale takeover, in the name of research and development, and their subordination to the logic and interests of Generation Now. For STEM belongs unequivocally to the present. There are histories of science, technology, engineering and mathematics, but there is no history of STEM.[3]

Having thus repudiated the past, STEM also has no future. Its claim, rather, is to *be* the future. That's why its metaphors of choice are 'state of the art' and 'the cutting edge'. It is a future incubated in cavernous, glass-walled enclosures ranging from research laboratories to corporate headquarters, or even giant domes designed for the simulation of natural ecosystems, their closely guarded and strictly controlled interiors masquerading as open access, disguising secrecy as transparency. The acronym is like a key-code that unlocks the door to the incubator. Only those in possession of the code can enter. And, to win possession, you have to be smart. This idea of smartness, which has gained extraordinary traction in recent years, connotes an intelligence that is quick in solving problems, as well as devious, giving its possessor a competitive edge over his or her more slow-witted rivals. It is the hallmark of the successful entrepreneur, often placed at the top in any list of attributes that a STEM-based education should inculcate in students exposed to it. The very purpose of such education, according to advocates, is to prepare the coming generation for a technocratic world order in which only the smart will survive.

Is there any place in a new order so skewed towards science and technology for the arts? In 2010, the Rhode Island School of Design (RISD) – one of the oldest colleges of art and design in the United States, and among the most prestigious in the world today – hit on the idea of adding A for 'arts' to STEM, thus turning it to STEAM. With this initiative, according to its own publicity, RISD aims to prepare future generations to compete in today's innovation economy.[4] The idea, which has since become mainstream, is to bring art and design into the frame as ways of thinking outside the box, which the STEM project requires to satisfy its insatiable thirst for innovation. In the marketplace of knowledge, novelty is a condition for competitive advantage, and artists and designers, known as creatives, are tasked with coming up with the new ideas the competition calls for, not just for the design of new knowledge products but for their advertisement. The effect, however, is to supercharge the already hyperbolic futurism of STEM, by including the arts within a championship for which students are to be trained, like Olympic athletes, to compete for the prize of success.

The Science and the arts

This marriage of artistic prowess with elite sport, however, may be a step too far even for advocates of progressive humanism, who see mirrored in the history of art a story of civilizational advance. For them, the arts are less accessory to science and technology than complementary, offering a space for self-expression alongside the overall improvement in living standards wrought by science and its applications.[5] Even the victorious in the cut-throat world of corporate competition would admit that their rise would be without meaning if the view from the top revealed nothing of intrinsic value. Is it not the role of the arts to widen our horizons, even to open hearts and minds to more fundamental truths? Might they even restore our faith in the Enlightenment project? A variety of arguments have been proposed to this effect. At their most trivial, they reduce the arts to entertainment, designed to fill the empty hours of affluent leisure. For some, art answers to a yearning for sublimity, mystery and wonder in a world otherwise so analysed that it has lost its power to enchant. For others, it is an index of cultural creativity, an acknowledgement of diversity, or a badge of civilization.

The logic of complementarity, however, while it confers upon the arts an intrinsic merit equal to that of the Science, does nothing to challenge STEM on its own ground. On the contrary, it reproduces a persistent dualism between affective, embodied experience and the cognitive operations of a disembodied intellect, or between aesthetic judgement and the work of reason, each furnished with its own distinctive style of creativity. Many patrons of the arts see the role of artistic endeavour as a necessary rebalancing, designed to temper the profiteering of the innovation economy with a human face and moral conscience. Indeed, a move along these lines has recently been proposed by no less august a body than the British Academy, the United Kingdom's national academy for the arts, humanities and social sciences. Seeking to emulate the success of STEM in attracting both public and private support, the Academy proposes a matching acronym, SHAPE, standing for 'social sciences, humanities and the arts for people and the economy'. Proponents of the acronym point to the perspectives that SHAPE disciplines can bring to bear to 'help us make sense of the human world', and to 'make innovation work harder for the benefit of everyone'.[6]

This only bolsters the innovation economy. Far from questioning the legitimacy of the Science, it offers a route for the arts, along with the humanities and social sciences, to get in on the act by sidling up to STEM in the hopes of siphoning off some of its accumulated largesse, and benefiting from its proximity to power. The world to which SHAPE commits is still a *human* world, and its interventions are still, and exclusively, for human benefit. SHAPE resembles STEM in that, unlike its component disciplines, it has no past, and no future. It is a creature of Generation Now. Yet the arts, in my view, have a far more radical role to play than as a mere complement to the Science. This is to recover the sense of correspondence, of going along with things and learning from them, that is repudiated by the logic of the acronym. The latter, as we have seen, cuts us off from the matters of which we speak, promoting an attitude that is at once disengaged and manipulative, epitomized by the word 'smart'. The practices of art, however, have the potential to foster precisely the opposite attitude: of enduring attention, responsiveness and care.

Could it be for the arts, then, to reverse the academic posture, to restore ways of knowing the world to ways of being in it, and thereby to rescue science, technology, engineering and mathematics from their STEM-induced stultification? This is not to oppose science to the arts, or to see them as complementing one another, but to ground both in the collaboration of generations. After all, for such giants as Vitruvius, Alberti, Leonardo and Constable – founding figures, respectively, in architecture, perspective, anatomy and meteorology – science and art were never separate or even separable endeavours, but rather long-standing traditions of inquiry, unified in their commitment to careful observation, patient experimentation, precise description and informed speculation. Indeed, this is how the real sciences, and real scientists, have always worked, and still work today, feeling their way from within, guided by genuine wonder, curiosity and wisdom. This calls, however, for an imagination wholly distinct from that of the kind coveted by STEM, or even by STEAM. It is an imagination that, far from closing in on smart solutions, opens up to the world's ceaseless becoming, drawing its creative powers from the self-same source. This is science not as innovation, but as longing.

Generation Now, however, sees it otherwise. The future, it insists, is a problem to be solved. And it invariably reaches to science, technology, engineering and mathematics for the tools to do so. It may call in artists and designers, as well, to conjure up a vision not only of the world to come, but also of the creatures destined to inhabit it. This is a vision that would pitch us headlong into a regime of artificial intelligence, virtual reality and fully automated work, in which mind and reason are finally set loose from their bodily and sensuous moorings, reducing the latter to empty husks. Human life itself, falling through the gap between outsourced minds and docile bodies, would be bound for extinction. Far from healing the rupture, instituted in the Enlightenment, between mind and world, or between reason and nature, this is to go to the opposite extreme. And for STEM-trained champions of posthumanity, the trend is unstoppable. It is inevitable, they argue, that humans will design themselves out of existence, by creating machines that exceed the intellectual capacities by the possession of which they had once defined themselves. Like it or not, we had better get ready for it.

Digitization and fingerwork

This prophecy is delusional. The fantasy of solving the future belongs to the same genre as the dream of transhumanism to solve death. It is, moreover, a dangerous delusion, since its pursuit can only leave a greater pile of ruination in its wake, making it more difficult, not less, for those who come after us to find their ways in the world. It would leave them with no trails to follow. There is, of course, nothing new in the prophecy itself, since, as we've seen, projections of this kind are an inevitable by-product of the idea of progress.[7] What is possibly new is the emergence of the technological means to place the projection within touching distance of realization. The promise of these means is to usher in a world beyond life and its labours, beyond the vital. This world will be *digital*. Offering powers of massive computation and instantaneous communication exceeding the wildest dreams of our ancestors, the digital revolution looks set – according to those who believe in it – to release intelligence, once and for all, from its housing in senescent and malfunctioning human bodies in periodic need of renewal. Generational replacement will be a thing of the past.

What the fantasy ignores are the demands the technology places, for it to function at all, upon the earth and its inhabitants. It ignores the labours of bodies enslaved, in massive numbers and often appalling conditions, to the extraction of heavy metals essential to digital operations. It ignores the energy requirements, and consequent emissions, of the supercomputers that keep the whole system running. It ignores the rocket power used to launch the thousands of communications satellites currently orbiting the planet. Finally, it ignores the toxic accumulations, on the earth and increasingly in space, of defunct devices. Poisoning the earth may not matter to a moneyed, technologically enabled elite whose dream is to escape from it, but it creates a nightmare for everyone else. How long the digital age will last is anyone's guess, though I am inclined to apply the 150-year rule. Coal's heyday lasted from the 1810s to the 1960s; the age of oil and gas began in the 1910s and will last perhaps until the 2060s. On that score, the digital era, starting in the 1980s, has until the 2130s. There is no knowing what will follow. Of one thing, however, we can be certain: digitization is not forever.

How, then, might we imagine a post-digital world? Though the days of the digital may be numbered, we can be fairly confident that those who come after us, a century or two from now, will still be possessed of eyes and ears, a voice, and a full complement of digits, consisting in their ten fingers. The facility of fingers to bend and curl with extraordinary precision has made it possible for ancestral human beings to make their mark in ways unmatched by creatures of any other kind. It has allowed the literate among them, in particular, to write by hand. In every line of writing, words spill out onto the surface of the page as the hand – now hesitating as it awaits coming thought, now rushing to catch up with it – leaves a meandering trail in its wake. The reader, in turn, is tasked with following the affect-laden twists and turns of the line with eyes that linger close to the surface. They may even trace the line with a finger while voicing the corresponding sounds, making it seem as if the page itself were speaking.[8] Could this offer a model for the reading and writing of generations to come?

Ironically, the fingerwork of handwriting was one of the first victims of digital technology. For, in substituting the keypad and the screen for the pen and the page, writing in the strict sense of inscribing a line on a surface became practically impossible. All you can do on a keypad is tap. With every tap, a discrete and standardized graphic element is brought up onscreen. To write, you have to assemble these elements into words and sentences, which encode the meanings you want to convey. This leaves the eye of the reader, with no line to follow and no surface on which to find purchase, having to cut through the screen, as through a windowpane, to retrieve the meanings lurking behind. But, once digitization has purged words of writing of the surface distractions of the letterline, why stop there? It is not hard to imagine that, after writing, speech will be digitization's next victim. Eventually, the affective powers of the voice will be banished from speaking, just as the keypad and screen have banished those of the hand from writing. Instead, digital synthesizers, operated by neurotransmitters from the brain, will pump out messages assembled from a standardized repertoire of speech sounds.

Stripped of the powers of manual and vocal expression, are we fated to go the same way as our technology, into mutually assured destruction? One little invention could save the day, and perhaps the planet too. It would consist of a hand-held tube, mounted in a shaft, and filled with a black liquid extract. The tube is closed at one end, while to the other is affixed a tip of keratin – the stuff of feathers and fingernails – sliced down the middle. On contact of the tip with a surface, capillary action draws the liquid down through the slit, so as to leave a trace. It is possible to write with this instrument on almost any even surface. Its versatility is unmatched by any contemporary digital interface. It costs almost nothing to make, from natural ingredients that can be obtained virtually anywhere. It is easy to use, requires no external energy source and leaves no pollution in its wake. This simple invention could secure the future of writing for millennia, as indeed it did until the forces of digitization drove it to the brink. As we relearn to write by means of this device, might we recover our voice as well?

Winding up

This chapter has ranged from acronymics to digitization. They may be different, but behind both lies the same logic. It is a logic that compresses linear movement – whether of studying, writing, speaking or simply living – into a scatter of points, flattened onto the plane of a present which, admitting to neither past nor future, is consequently drained of affect. The similarity to the logic of the genealogical model, introduced in Chapter 1, is striking. Given that the model is equally rooted in the perspective of Generation Now, however, it comes as no surprise. But, just as we found an alternative to the genealogic in lineages of begetting, so the remedies we propose for acronymics and digitization offer ways for life to carry on, with the potential to heal the rupture between reason and nature, mind and world. For acronymics, the remedy is to foster the arts, neither as accessory to the Science nor as a complement to it, but as a means to reinstate science's commitment to intergenerational collaboration in the disciplined work of observation, experimentation and description – that is, to *research* in the strict sense of 'searching again', retracing the paths of ancestors in an original movement of renewal.[9]

In the case of digitization, however, our remedy lies in a reprise of older ways of writing, and of speaking. Historically, of course, humans were speaking long before they began to write in any recognizable script. But for generations to come, it might just be the other way around. The liberation of the hand and its digits from the tyranny of the keypad and touchscreen could flow through into the voice, releasing its poetic and prosodic qualities – or in a word, its *response-ability* – which rampant digitization had previously earmarked for extinction. The lullaby and the lament, which once accompanied the passage of a life from cradle to grave, along with the practices of naming that voiced it into being, would be revived – not as recorded heritage, conserved in the digital archive, but as living tradition. Writing that issues from the dexterous fingerwork of the thinking hand would reopen the door to speaking that wells up on the breath, in sounds sculpted by the tongue and lips. And as we retrieve our pen to write, perhaps we'll also recall the ploughman of old, whose pages are his fields, turning the soil in the revolutions of the agricultural cycle.[10]

Lest all this should sound like a forlorn attempt to wind back the clock, steeped in a syrup of nostalgia, let me stress that what is at stake here is not regression but realignment. My objection is to the belief that there is no way forward save by *breaking through*, from one level to the next. The temptation, among those who think like this, is to suppose that the final breakthrough is either imminent or under way at this very moment, marking the fulfilment of humankind's historical destiny. Humans will momentarily become masters of the earth only to discover that, in doing so, they have released forces, of a magnitude beyond their control, which threaten oblivion. In recent decades, the Science has come up with a novel and seductive cloak for this story to wear. We are entering a new epoch in the history of the earth, it tells us – namely, the Anthropocene. The term is controversial, not least in its tarring of all humans with the same brush. Surely, not everyone is complicit in a story that, historically, has produced more slaves than masters. But it is not the *Anthropos* that troubles me so much as the *-cene*.

Geologists unfold the story of the earth as a sequence of epochs, of which the most recent, together making up the Quaternary period, are the Pleistocene, the Holocene and now the Anthropocene. It is hardly a coincidence that, in this story, the Holocene coincides with the span of human history, bookended by the era of 'early man' in the Pleistocene, before history began, and the new epoch of the Anthropocene which brings history to an end. Much effort has gone into selecting a signal to index the start of the Anthropocene, a so-called golden spike which could be identified in strata around the world. Could it be microplastics, concrete residues, soot from power stations, accumulations of broiler chicken bones or radioactive fallout from nuclear weapons testing? One spike, however, doesn't make an epoch. The real question is: what comes after? If the Anthropocene were really an epoch, then for there to be life afterwards we would have to project another spike, untold millions of years from now, marking the moment when the earth's remaining creatures, be they recognizably human or of any other kinds, break through to the far side. But what if the Anthropocene is not really an epoch at all?

Let's not forget the Angel of History. What he sees is not a new epoch opening up ahead but a ruin left behind, deposited upon the plane of the present, and visible in the scars inflicted upon the landscape by the stuttering march of progress. If the Anthropocene is a ruin rather than an epoch, then life afterwards comes from turning your back on it or putting it behind you, precisely as the Angel has done, to regain the ways of predecessors. That's what I mean by realignment. A future beyond the Anthropocene, I contend, can only lie in relearning how to go along *with* the elements that sustain all of existence, as our ancestors once did, and as plants and animals still do. But prioritizing the regeneration of human life and its coexistence with other planetary beings over genealogical inheritance and replacement may mean putting science and technology to one side. The future is not, after all, a problem to be solved. It is, rather, the life we long for, both for ourselves and for generations to come. And to reach for it will mean turning once again to the time-honoured themes of filiation and begetting, kinship and descent.

Notes

1 Generations and the Regeneration of Life

1 King James Bible, Genesis, ch. 5.

2 As anthropologist Gisli Palsson puts it, 'Naming is a speech act shaping the life course and the person involved': Gisli Palsson, 'Ensembles of biosocial relations', in *Biosocial Becomings: Integrating Social and Biological Anthropology*, ed. Tim Ingold and Gisli Palsson, Cambridge University Press, 2013, pp. 22–41, p. 33. See also *The Anthropology of Names and Naming*, ed. Barbara Bodenhorn and Gabriele vom Bruck, Cambridge University Press, 2006.

3 These conventions, along with detailed instructions on how to construct genealogical charts, can be found in John Barnes, 'Genealogies', in *The Craft of Social Anthropology*, ed. A. L. Epstein, London: Tavistock, 1967, pp. 101–27.

4 That is why the model should on no account be confused with the story. To critique the model is absolutely not, as anthropologist Philippe Descola thinks, to accuse peoples who attribute great importance to genealogical

relations of succumbing to a 'Western perversity'. See Phillipe Descola, *Beyond Nature and Culture*, trans. Janet Lloyd, University of Chicago Press, 2013, p. 333; and for a rejoinder, Tim Ingold, 'A naturalist abroad in the museum of ontology: Philippe Descola's *Beyond Nature and Culture*', *Anthropological Forum*, 2016, 26(3): 301–20, pp. 317–18.

5 In the only diagram to appear in Darwin's masterwork *On the Origin of Species*, the modification and diversification of species along lines of descent is depicted schematically as transiting a sequence of horizontal bands, each taken to stand for an arbitrary interval of 1,000 generations. Significantly, Darwin drew every phylogenetic line as a rectilinear series of dots. He was right to do so, since, in the dotted line, all movement is collapsed into its constituent points. The line itself is lifeless and inert. See Charles Darwin, *On the Origin of Species by Means of Natural Selection, or the Preservation of Favoured Races in the Struggle for Life* (reprint of 1st edn of 1859), London: Watts, 1950, pp. 90–1. On the dotted line, see Tim Ingold, *Lines: A Brief History*, London: Routledge, 2007, p. 94.

6 Jacques Monod, *Chance and Necessity*, trans. Austryn Wainhouse, London: Collins, 1972, p. 110.

7 See, for example, Christophe Boesch and Michael Tomasello, 'Chimpanzee and human cultures', *Current Anthropology*, 1998, 39(5): 591–614; and Andrew Whiten, Nicola McGuigan, Sarah Marshall-Pescini and Lydia M. Hopper, 'Emulation, imitation, over-imitation and the scope of culture for child and chimpanzee', *Philosophical Transactions of the Royal Society*, Series B, 2009, 364: 2417–28.

8 See, for example, Robert Boyd and Peter J. Richerson,

Culture and the Evolutionary Process, University of Chicago Press, 1985; William H. Durham, *Coevolution: Genes, Culture and Human Diversity*, Stanford University Press, 1991; Peter Richerson and Robert Boyd, *Not by Genes Alone: How Culture Transformed Human Evolution*, University of Chicago Press, 2008; Robert A. Paul, *Mixed Messages: Cultural and Genetic Inheritance in the Constitution of Human Society*, University of Chicago Press, 2015. For an overview, see Tim Lewens, *Cultural Evolution: Conceptual Challenges*, Oxford University Press, 2015.

9 The literature on all this is far too extensive to list here. For a critical review, see Tim Ingold, 'Evolution without inheritance: steps to an ecology of learning', *Current Anthropology*, 2022, 63 (supplement 25): S32–S55.

10 For a devastating critique, see Susan Oyama, *The Ontogeny of Information: Developmental Systems and Evolution*, Cambridge University Press, 1985.

11 Ludwig Wittgenstein, *Philosophical Investigations*, Oxford: Blackwell, 1953, §11.

12 Henri Bergson, *Creative Evolution*, trans. Arthur Mitchell, London: Macmillan, 1922, p. 135. The emphasis is mine. I shall return to the gesture of leaning over, especially in Chapter 7.

13 Bergson, *Creative Evolution*, p. 45.

2 Modelling the Human Life Course

1 Walter Benjamin, 'Theses on the philosophy of history', in *Illuminations: Essays and Reflections*, ed. Hannah Arendt, trans. Harry Zohn, New York: Schocken Books, 1968, pp. 253–64, pp. 257–8.

2 The concept of the 'basic tripartitioning of the life

course', into phases of (1) education and preparation for work, (2) active employment, and (3) retirement, was first proposed in 1986 by social historian Martin Kohli. See Martin Kohli, 'The world we forgot: a historical review of the life course', in *Later Life: The Social Psychology of Aging*, ed. Victor W. Marshall, Newbury Park, CA: Sage Publications, 1986, pp. 271–303, p. 280. The effect of this 'institutional age segregation', as sociologists Gunhild O. Hagestad and Peter Uhlenberg report, is that people in each of the three phases spend time only with one another, to the exclusion of those in other phases. 'Children and youth are channeled into daycare and schools where they spend most of the day with a narrow band of age peers. For adults, days are anchored in work settings that exclude the young and the old. And older people, who have limited access to school and work sites, are expected to live retired lives of leisure.' See Gunhild O. Hagestad and Peter Uhlenberg, 'The social separation of old and young: a root of ageism', *Journal of Social Issues*, 2005, 61(2): 343–60, p. 346.

3   See Chapter 7, p. 107.

4   On how state formation and changes in the organization of labour have restructured the life course, see Karl Ulrich Mayer and Urs Schoepflin, 'The state and the life course', *Annual Review of Sociology*, 1989, 15: 187–209.

5   Jeanette Lykkegård, *This Is Our Life: Living and Dying among the Chukchi of Northern Kamchatka*, doctoral dissertation, School of Culture and Society, University of Aarhus, 2019, p. 160.

6   Bergson, *Creative Evolution*, p. 134.

7   Gilbert Simondon, 'The genesis of the individual', trans.

Mark Cohen and Sanford Kwinter, in *Incorporations*, ed. Jonathan Crary and Sanford Kwinter, New York: Zone, 1992, pp. 297–319, p. 300.

8 Benjamin, 'Theses on the philosophy of history', pp. 253–4.

9 For an excellent discussion of transhumanism, see Norman Wirzba, *This Sacred Life: Humanity's Place in a Wounded World*, Cambridge University Press, 2021, pp. 34–60.

10 John Wyon Burrow, *Evolution and Society: A Study in Victorian Social Theory*, Cambridge University Press, 1966, p. 227.

3 Remembering the Way

1 These and the following thoughts have been much inspired by the recent volume *Pathways: Exploring the Routes of a Movement Heritage*, edited by Daniel Svensson, Katarina Saltzman and Sverker Sörlin, Winwick, Cambs.: White Horse Press, 2022.

2 I have discussed the formation of the palimpsest at greater length in an essay entitled 'Palimpsest: ground and page', in my collection *Imagining for Real: Essays on Creation, Attention and Correspondence*, London: Routledge, 2022, pp. 180–98.

3 Robert Pogue Harrison, *The Dominion of the Dead*, University of Chicago Press, 2003, pp. x–xi. Jason Taylor and Robert Miner discuss Vico's etymology of 'human' in a footnote to their recent translation of *The New Science*, New Haven, CT: Yale University Press, 2020, p. 12.

4 In a recent article on the challenges faced by coastal villagers in the island of Fiji, threatened by rising sea-levels, in moving their settlements to higher ground

inland, Kate Lyons notes that, for many, burial sites are the biggest obstacle to relocation. Should they leave the dead behind, only for them to be washed away, or should their bones be exhumed and taken to the new site? Either alternative, as Lyons notes, 'is deeply traumatic'. The problem lies not in the loss of the past. It is rather that, without ancestors to light their path, there is no hope for the future. Kate Lyons, 'How to move a country: Fiji's radical plan to escape rising sea-levels', *The Guardian Long Read*, 8 November 2022: www.theguardian.com/environment/2022/nov/08/how-to-move-a-country-fiji-radical-plan-escape-rising-seas-climate-crisis.

5 Erin Manning, 'What things do when they shape each other: the way of the anarchive': http://s3.amazonaws.com/arena-attachments/990937/bdabcf14b7f9b5ab91be88ac871d44aa.pdf?1493056093, p. 8.

6 I am most grateful to Hong Wan Chan for permission to refer to her work, which is still in progress, including her papers 'Recovering obscured experiences of landscape in Nanhai, China', presented at the Under the Landscape Symposium, Santorini and Therasia, Greece, 26–29 June 2022, organized by Boulouki, Itinerant Workshop on Traditional Building Techniques; and 'Tracing the lineage in a modernizing landscape: five diptychs of a village in the Pearl River Delta, China', in *Remediated Maps: Transmedial Approaches to Cartographic Imagination*, ed. Tommaso Morawski and Tanja Michalsky, Rome: Campisano Editore (Quaderni della Bibliotheca Hertziana), 2023. Chan's family history offers powerful testimony to the consequences of flattening a landscape that once teemed with burgeoning lineages. However, its anarchival powers

are not yet completely suppressed. Even today, in apparent defiance of the order of the cemetery with its zones, rows and numbered plots, people still celebrate at the graves of their ancestors, setting off fireworks and releasing smoke from burned paper offerings.

7 Tuck Po Lye, 'Knowledge, Forest, and Hunter-Gatherer Movement: The Batek of Pahang, Malaysia', doctoral dissertation, University of Hawai'i, 1997, p. 372.

8 Bergson, *Creative Evolution*, p. 17.

9 Lye, 'Knowledge, Forest, and Hunter-Gatherer Movement', p. 149.

4 Uncertainty and Possibility

1 Juvenilization, as Harrison argues, is the very opposite of rejuvenation. Whereas rejuvenation 'gives the past a future to grow into', juvenilization 'militates against historicity and deprives the present of temporal and phenomenological depth . . . It gives youth a premature old age, and old age a callow youthfulness': Robert Pogue Harrison, *Juvenescence: A Cultural History of Our Age*, University of Chicago Press, 2014, p. 116.

2 This may also account for the perception that generational spans are getting shorter, and their turnover accelerating, to the point that one has scarcely made its presence felt before the next is at its heels. If the span of every generation is half that of the one before, then the succession of generations will tend towards an absolute limit. I am grateful to one of the reviewers of my original manuscript for this observation.

3 Here, and in the following sections of this chapter, I draw on my already published article, 'Uncertainty and possibility / Incertitude et possibilité', *In Analysis*, 2022, 6(1): 10–18.

4 Clifford Geertz, *The Interpretation of Cultures*, New York: Basic Books, 1973, p. 45.

5 This is an expression, according to Myers, common to many Aboriginal peoples of the Western Desert: Fred R. Myers, *Pintupi Country, Pintupi Self: Sentiment, Place and Politics among Western Desert Aborigines*, Washington, DC: Smithsonian University Press, 1986, p. 53.

6 Myers, *Pintupi Country, Pintupi Self*, p. 53.

7 It is worth contrasting this Aboriginal veneration for ancestors, as world-creators who laid down the paths for their successors to follow, with the advice contained in a recently published, popular manual, targeted at modern Western readers, on how to be a good ancestor. According to its author, Roman Krznaric, humans are innately endowed with 'acorn brains', which make them the only species capable of imagining alternatives that project far into the future. To be good ancestors, we should make best use of the capacity of these brains to think in the long term. 'We are *Homo prospectus*', he says; 'the ape that looks forward'. Evidently the author, as a paid-up representative of Generation Now, has looked into the mirror of nature and seen his own reflection in the figure of this ape. Roman Krznaric, *The Good Ancestor: How to Think Long Term in a Short-Term World*, London: W. H. Allen, 2020.

8 I refer in particular to Dewey's essay of 1934, 'Art as experience', in *John Dewey: The Later Works, 1925–1953*, Vol. X: *1934*, ed. Jo Ann Boydston, Carbondale: Southern Illinois University Press, 1987, pp. 42–110.

9 Dewey, 'Art as experience', p. 50.

10 This was in a later lecture, dating from 1938, and

published as *Experience and Education*, New York: Free Press, 2015, p. 35.

11 James J. Gibson, *The Ecological Approach to Visual Perception*, Hillsdale, NJ: Lawrence Erlbaum, 1986. Quotations in this paragraph are from pp. 245 and 254.

12 Jan Masschelein, 'E-ducating the gaze: the idea of a poor pedagogy', *Ethics and Education*, 2010, 5: 43–53, p. 46.

13 I return to this idea of education in Chapter 7, p. 100.

14 Tim Ingold, *The Life of Lines*, London: Routledge, 2015, pp. 138–42.

15 Erin Manning, *The Minor Gesture*, Durham, NC: Duke University Press, 2016, pp. 6, 117–18.

16 Dewey, 'Art as experience', p. 59.

17 Karl Popper, *The Open Society and its Enemies*, Princeton University Press, 1950.

18 Tim Ingold, 'On human correspondence', *Journal of the Royal Anthropological Institute*, 2017, 23: 9–27.

19 From Rilke's *Uncollected Poems*, extracted from *A Year with Rilke: Daily Readings from the Best of Rainer Maria Rilke*, ed. and trans. Joanna Macy and Anita Barrows, New York: Harper Collins, 2009, p. 7.

5 Loss and Extinction

1 Alastair Reid, 'Growing, flying, happening', in his *Barefoot: The Collected Poems*, ed. Tom Pow, Cambridge: Galileo, 2018, pp. 87–8, p. 88. I have highlighted the word 'astonishment' in order to emphasize the contrast with 'surprise', discussed in Chapter 4.

2 Titus Lucretius Carus, *De rerum natura*, ed. William Ellery Leonard: www.perseus.tufts.edu/hopper/text?doc=Perseus%3Atext%3A1999.02.0131.

3 See my poem 'On extinction', in Tim Ingold, *Correspondences*, Cambridge: Polity, 2020, pp. 148–51.

4 George Gaylord Simpson, 'The species concept', *Evolution*, 1951, 5(4): 285–98, p. 289.

5 Karl Marx, *Economic and Political Manuscripts of 1844*, trans. Martin Milligan, revised by Dirk J. Struik, transcribed by Andy Blunden, 2000: www.marxists.org/archive/marx/works/download/pdf/Economic-Philosophic-Manuscripts-1844.pdf, p. 31. The emphasis is mine.

6 Thom van Dooren, *Flight Ways: Life and Loss at the Edge of Extinction*, New York: Columbia University Press, 2014; 'Spectral crows in Hawai'i: conservation and the work of inheritance', in *Extinction Studies: Stories of Time, Death and Generations*, ed. Deborah Bird Rose, Thom van Dooren and Matthew Chrulew, New York: Columbia University Press, 2017, pp. 187–215, p. 193.

7 van Dooren, 'Spectral crows in Hawai'i', p. 188.

8 Here is the problem passage in full: 'Evolution by natural selection – that great engine of new ways of life – is grounded in forms of inheritance that simultaneously retain the achievements of the past while constantly transforming them to produce new variability. This variability arises through recombination, mutation, and other forms of transformation'; van Dooren, 'Spectral crows in Hawai'i', p. 202.

9 Eric Wolf, 'Perilous ideas: race, culture, people', *Current Anthropology*, 1994, 35(1): 1–12, p. 1.

10 *Oxford English Dictionary*, 'race', n.6.

11 *Oxford English Dictionary*, 'race', n.6, I. 1. a. 1676.

12 Charles Darwin, *The Descent of Man; and Selection*

in Relation to Sex (new edn), New York: D. Appleton and Company, 1889, pp. 128 and 132.

13 Darwin, *The Descent of Man*, p. 182.

14 Darwin, *The Descent of Man*, p. 156.

15 Arthur Keith, *The Place of Prejudice in Modern Civilization*, London: Williams & Norgate, 1931, p. 49.

16 For a comprehensive review of the Neanderthal debate in palaeoanthropology, see Paul Graves, 'New models and metaphors for the Neanderthal debate', *Current Anthropology*, 1991, 32: 513–41. 'Most participants in the debate', as Graves notes (p. 525), 'cannot resist a simplistic metaphor of European colonialism and the analogies which are drawn from it. Indeed, the whole concept of displacement without admixture and the evolution of "an entirely new species" carries with it the implication of progressive trends which we owe to 19th-century ideologies.'

17 In a census of 2011, more than 19,000 Tasmanians identified as Aboriginal people: www.britannica.com /topic/Tasmanian.

18 Marx, *Economic and Political Manuscripts*, p. 31.

19 I refer to the naturalist Sir David Attenborough, whose programmes on the natural world have attracted global audiences in their millions.

20 For an excellent discussion of these dilemmas of conservation, see Andrew Whitehouse, 'Anthropological approaches to conservation conflicts', in *Conflicts in Conservation: Navigating towards Solutions*, ed. Stephen M. Redpath, R. J. Gutiérrez, Kevin A. Wood and Juliette C. Young, Cambridge University Press, pp. 94–104.

6 Recentring Anthropos

1 *The Human Revolution: Behavioural and Biological Perspectives on the Origins of Modern Humans*, ed. Paul Mellars and Chris Stringer, Edinburgh University Press, 1989.

2 For example, *Social Life of Early Man*, ed. Sherwood L. Washburn, London: Methuen, 1962.

3 L. P. Hartley, *The Go-Between*, Harmondsworth: Hamish Hamilton, 1953.

4 Tim Ingold, *The Life of Lines*, London: Routledge, pp. 115–19.

5 Here I follow Anthony Bonner's translation: 'man is a manifying animal', in *Selected Works of Ramon Llull (1232–1316)*, Vol. I, ed. and trans. Anthony Bonner, Princeton University Press, 1985, p. 609.

6 Alfred North Whitehead, *Religion in the Making: Lowell Lectures 1926*, Cambridge University Press, 1926, p. 102.

7 This has been particularly shown to be the case for the region of Amazonia. Once thought to be a sparsely populated and largely pristine wilderness, studies have revealed, to the contrary, that in pre-Columbian times it was a major centre of crop cultivation, supporting many millions of people and at least eighty-three native domesticated species. See Charles R. Clement, William M. Denevan, Michael J. Heckenberger, André Braga Junqueira, Eduardo G. Neves, Wenceslau G. Teixeira and William I. Woods, 'The domestication of Amazonia before European conquest', *Proceedings of the Royal Society*, Series B, 2015, 282: 20150813: http://dx.doi.org/10.1098/rspb.2015.0813.

8 Tim Ingold and Elizabeth Hallam, 'Creativity and cultural improvisation: an introduction', in *Creativity and*

Cultural Improvisation, ed. Elizabeth Hallam and Tim Ingold, Oxford: Berg, 2007, pp. 1–24, p. 10.

9 Harrison, *Juvenescence*, pp. 97 and 113. There is much common ground between Harrison's position and the argument I lay out in these pages. I share his view that Western civilization is constitutionally afflicted by periodic loss of memory, the disavowal of what it sees as the past, and the consequent surrender of its achievements to ruin (p. 49), although for Harrison this is no mere disease of modernity but can be traced back to Classical Greece. Above all, however, I am with Harrison in insisting that begetting – or what he calls 'birthing the new from the womb of antecedence' – entails a retrieval of old ways 'that has little to do with revival and everything to do with revitalization' (p. 113).

10 See Chapter 4, pp. 54–5.

11 One particular conflict concerns the Storheia and Roan wind farms, located on the Fosen peninsula in central Norway. In October 2021, by which time the farms had been built and following a petition from local Sámi herders, Norway's Supreme Court ruled that they violated the herders' rights under international conventions, leading to demands that the 151 turbines should be torn down, along with the many miles of roads built to facilitate their construction. At the time of writing, the matter remains unresolved. See www .reuters.com/business/environment/norway-wind-tur bines-should-be-torn-down-reindeer-herders-say-2021 -11-12.

12 Geographer Hayden Lorimer offers a particularly fine account of the conjoint reading of the wind by reindeer and their herdsmen, in a study of herding in Scotland's

Cairngorm Mountains. See Hayden Lorimer, 'Herding memories of humans and animals', *Environment and Planning D: Society and Space*, 2006, 24: 497–518.

7 The Way of Education

1 Immanuel Kant, 'A translation of the introduction to Kant's *Physische Geographie*', in *Kant's Concept of Geography and Its Relation to Recent Geographical Thought*, by J. A. May, University of Toronto Press, 1970, pp. 255–64, p. 257.

2 This argument is inspired by the work of Gert Biesta, *Letting Art Teach: Art Education 'after' Joseph Beuys*, Arnhem: Artez Press, 2017. I return to Biesta's ideas below (p. 101).

3 The word comes from an influential text co-authored by activist and educational theorist Stefano Harney, with poet and literary scholar Fred Moten, entitled *The Undercommons: Fugitive Planning and Black Study*, Wivenhoe: Minor Compositions, 2013.

4 See Chapter 4, p. 62. On understanding versus undercommoning, see Tim Ingold, *Anthropology and/as Education*, London: Routledge, 2018, p. 38.

5 On ageing and begetting, see Chapter 2, pp. 118–19.

6 See Chapter 4, p. 57.

7 Masschelein, 'E-ducating the gaze', p. 50.

8 See John Cage, *Silence: Lectures and Writings by John Cage* (50th anniversary edition), Middletown, CT: Wesleyan University Press, 2011, p. 10; Donna Haraway, *Staying with the Trouble: Making Kin in the Chthulucene*, Durham, NC: Duke University Press, 2016, p. 105; Gert Biesta, *Beyond Learning: Democratic Education for a Human Future*, Boulder, CO: Paradigm, 2006, p. 70.

9 Alfonso Lingis, *The Community of Those Who Have Nothing in Common*, Bloomington: Indiana University Press, 1994.

10 Hannah Arendt, 'The crisis in education', The Humanities Institute, University of California, Santa Cruz: https://thi.ucsc.edu/wp-content/uploads/2016/09/Arendt-Crisis_In_Education-1954.pdf, p. 5. See also Chapter 2, pp. 28–9.

11 Though the theme of love for the world, *amor mundi*, runs through all of Arendt's work, she rarely addressed it directly. However, in a letter to her former teacher and friend Karl Jaspers, dated 6 August 1955, Arendt wrote: 'I've begun so late, really only in recent years, to truly love the world . . . Out of gratitude, I want to call my book on political theories "Amor Mundi"' (cited in Lucy Tatman, 'Arendt and Augustine: more than one kind of love', *Sophia*, 2013, 52: 625–35, p. 626). She appears to have dropped the idea, however, since the book was eventually published, in 1958, under the title *The Human Condition* (Chicago University Press).

12 Arendt, 'The crisis in education', p. 13.

13 Arendt, 'The crisis in education', p. 10.

14 Arendt, 'The crisis in education', p. 8.

15 On the distinction between order-words and passwords, see Gilles Deleuze and Félix Guattari, *A Thousand Plateaus: Capitalism and Schizophrenia*, trans. Brian Massumi, London: Continuum, 2004, p. 122.

16 This paragraph draws extensively on an equivalent passage in my essay 'The world in a basket', in *Imagining for Real*, pp. 277–8. It was writing the essay, above all, that led me to the idea for this book.

17 Harrison, *Juvenescence*, p. 130.

18 'Mathematics', as biochemist and theoretician of chaos Otto Rössler once remarked, 'is no more than pottery'. He might just as well have said that pottery is no less than mathematics. Cited in Elizabeth de Freitas, 'Material encounters and media events: what kind of mathematics can a body do?' *Educational Studies in Mathematics*, 2016, 91: 185–202, p. 188.

8 After Science and Technology

1 See p. 7.

2 Etymologically, 'philosophy' combines the Ancient Greek *philo-*, 'loving', and *sophis*, 'wise, learned'.

3 Harrison, too, has noted a tendency in modern science for both visionaries and ordinary practitioners to turn their backs on traditions of inquiry going back thousands of years, and to spurn the wisdom they embody as founded in ignorance. Even the last generation's theories 'may as well belong to the annals of prehistory'. Though this 'cultivated amnesia' is an inevitable by-product of the idea of progress through conjecture and refutation, my sense is that it has been massively exacerbated since the turn of the millennium, with the rise of STEM. See Harrison, *Juvenescence*, p. 51.

4 The relevant passage on the RISD website reads as follows: 'RISD has long valued the symbiosis between the arts and sciences, weaving cross-disciplinary exploration into various studio practices. In 2010, the college began to champion the addition of art and design to the national agenda of STEM (science, technology, engineering, math) education and research to develop a comprehensive educational model that would better prepare future generations to compete in the 21st-century innovation economy' –

www.risd.edu/academics/public-engagement. See also Anne Pirrie, 'Where science ends, art begins? Critical perspectives on the development of STEAM in the New Climatic Regime', in *Why Science and Art Creativities Matter: (Re-)Configuring STEAM for Future-Making Education*, ed. Pamela Burnard and Laura Colucci-Gray, Leiden: Brill, 2020, pp. 19–34.

5 This echoes the complementarity of academic and non-academic subjects discussed in Chapter 7, p. 97.

6 See www.thebritishacademy.ac.uk/this-is-shape.

7 See Chapter 2, p. 33.

8 This is how the monks of medieval Europe would read their liturgical texts, listening to the 'voices of the pages' (*voces paginarum*) they themselves would utter, and allowing the words to 'fall out' from the performance. See David Olson, *The World on Paper: The Conceptual and Cognitive Implications of Writing and Reading*, Cambridge University Press, 1994, pp. 184–5; Guglielmo Cavallo and Roger Chartier, 'Introduction', in *A History of Reading in the West*, ed. Guglielmo Cavallo and Roger Chartier, trans. Lydia G. Cochrane, Amherst: University of Massachusetts Press, 1999, pp. 1–36, pp. 17–18.

9 On the meaning of 'research', see Ingold, *Anthropology and/as Education*, pp. 71–4.

10 On the parallels between pen and plough, and between page and field, see Chapter 3, p. 42.

Index

Index

Index

Index

Index

Index